Quality's Greatest Hits

Classic Wisdom from the Leaders of Quality

Also available from ASQ Quality Press

Quality Quotes
Helio Gomez

101 Good Ideas: How to Improve Just about Any Process
Karen Bemowski and Brad Stratton, editors

Success through Quality: Support Guide for the Journey to
Continuous Improvement
Timothy J. Clark

Puzzling Quality Puzzles
J. P. Russell and Janice Russell

The Quality Toolbox
Nancy R. Tague

Business Process Improvement Toolbox
Bjørn Andersen

To request a complimentary catalog of ASQ Quality Press publications, call
800-248-1946, or visit our Online Bookstore at http://qualitypress.asq.org .

Quality's Greatest Hits

Classic Wisdom
from the Leaders of Quality

Zigmund Bluvband

ASQ Quality Press
Milwaukee, Wisconsin

Quality's Greatest Hits: Classic Wisdom from the Leaders of Quality
Zigmund Bluvband

Library of Congress Cataloging-in-Publication Data

Bluvband, Zigmund, 1947–
  Quality's greatest hits : classic wisdom from the leaders of quality /
Zigmund Bluvband.
    p. cm.
  Includes bibliographical references and index.
  ISBN 0-87389-531-2 (soft cover : alk. paper)
  1. Management—Quotations, maxims, etc. 2. Management. I. Title.

HD31 .B556 2002
658.4'013—dc21   2002003683

Note: As used in this document, the term "ISO 9000:2000" and all derivatives refer
to the ANSI/ISO/ASQ Q9000-2000 series of documents. All quotations come from
the American National Standard adoptions of these International Standards.

10 9 8 7 6 5 4 3 2 1

ISBN 0-87389-531-2

Acquisitions Editor: Annemieke Koudstaal
Project Editor: Craig S. Powell
Production Administrator: Gretchen Trautman
Special Marketing Representative: David Luth

ASQ Mission: The American Society for Quality advances individual,
organizational, and community excellence worldwide through learning,
quality improvement, and knowledge exchange.

Attention Bookstores, Wholesalers, Schools, and Corporations: ASQ Quality
Press books, videotapes, audiotapes, and software are available at quantity
discounts with bulk purchases for business, educational, or instructional use.
For information, please contact ASQ Quality Press at 800-248-1946, or write to
ASQ Quality Press, P.O. Box 3005, Milwaukee, WI 53201-3005.

To place orders or to request a free copy of the ASQ Quality Press Publications
Catalog, including ASQ membership information, call 800-248-1946. Visit our
Web site at www.asq.org or http://qualitypress.asq.org .

Printed in the United States of America

♾ Printed on acid-free paper

American Society for Quality

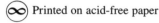

Quality Press
600 N. Plankinton Avenue
Milwaukee, Wisconsin 53203
Call toll free 800-248-1946
Fax 414-272-1734
www.asq.org
http://qualitypress.asq.org
http://standardsgroup.asq.org
E-mail: authors@asq.org

To "2S" in my life—my mother Sophia and my wife Sylvia—
the two women who made my life "2H"—happen and happy.

Table of Contents

Part II: Improvement Tools and Techniques

Part III: Probability and Statistics

Part IV: Reliability and Risk Assessment

Part V: Software

Part VI: Audit and Inspection

Foreword

It seems to me that the first set of "greatest hits" in history survives in the Bible, in its eminent set of rules of behavior entitled the Ten Commandments. This declaration of principles set a precedent that has been emulated for generations. Since then, a seemingly endless number of people have tried to imitate Moses by conceiving rules and formulating definitions, labeling them "business and life principles."

Using lists that outline rules of behavior has become the fashion today. This is especially evident in the endeavor to compile guidelines, replete with buzzwords, into guides for practitioners in various management fields. The best of these guides are extremely useful and enlightening. Some even offer a collection of quality management maxims.

Not only are there lists made up of ten rules—such a lovely number—but we also frequently encounter lists that are groups of seven or fourteen (double seven) rules. This is probably another rule that will soon be added to somebody's list. Indeed, everyone knows the seven basic tools, the seven new management and planning tools, the seven Baldrige criteria categories, the 7-S, and the seven deadly diseases that management must cure, as well as Crosby's fourteen-step approach to quality improvement and Deming's fourteen obligations of top management.

For years I have worked as a quality management consultant and as a teacher. In the course of these years, I have put together a collection, or potpourri if you will, of such definitions, principles, recipes, and "rules of thumb," writing down those recommendations that I deem effective, useful, and successful. I finally decided to organize these valuable ideas into an anthology of great thoughts, meanings, and definitions. That is how this book was created.

This book is unique: it may be the first guide to quality management thinking that at the same time reminds the professional about well-known but forgotten sources of information. The book sometimes offers step-by-step guidance on an important topic and sometimes makes only quick reference to a source. Some ideas and recipes contradict one another, some are similar, and some are only partially correlated. I have not judged and have not chosen the "best" or the "most frequently used" ones; instead, I have tried to present every expression and consideration I find helpful, creative, or just original. So, for those of us who care about quality and want to get some ideas, who want to trace the history of some great thoughts, or who want to become familiar with a principle offered by some big name (or not-so-big name), this book has many uses—and one of them may even be pure enjoyment.

The reader may simply go through the book and enjoy the outlook, glancing at every quotation, piece of advice, and interpretation. Alternatively, and complementarily, this book will introduce the reader to many great books, papers, and outstanding authors whose remarkable methodologies, sets of directions, and aphorisms have made an impact on quality management.

If there are any mistakes, they are mine alone, and I apologize. Please feel free to comment on anything you read.

Write to zigmund@qualitywisdom.com .

Zigmund Bluvband

How to Use This Book

"Quality is a people business," Phil Crosby once said. That's why this book is extremely important to almost all of us:

- Managers seeking a slogan to motivate workers

- Engineers looking for help or solutions

- Executives seeking the way of success

- CQM, Six Sigma Blackbelt, or CQE exam applicants hoping to refresh their memory or find information

- Any busy person looking for bathroom, home, or office "one-glance" reading

The book is divided into six parts:

- Management and General Wisdom

- Improvement Tools and Techniques

- Probability and Statistics

- Reliability and Risk Assessment

- Software

- Audit and Inspection

Each part is subdivided into chapters in which quotations and other material are organized by the numerical principle in accordance with the number of steps or points they contain; for example, *One of a kind* by W. Edwards Deming, *Two Qs* adapted from Joseph M. Juran and Frank M. Gryna, *Three-mu checklist of* kaizen *activities, IEEE's set of four common design views,* and *Five steps of customer-driven organizations.*

This numerical rule has been chosen both for the sake of a more memorable way of presentation—to avoid "beating about the bush"—and for the convenience of those who are pressed for time and just need a telegraphic tip or two on some topic. After all, "brevity is the soul of wit."

If, for example, one remembers the number seven in reference to management diseases, then it will be no trouble at all to open to "7" in part I, "Management and General Wisdom," and refresh in one's memory the "seven deadly diseases that management must cure," as well as the name of their famous author, W. Edwards Deming.

I have tried to find a suitable title for each entry, one that conveys the whole idea of the entry in a nutshell and will enable the reader to easily find it using the extensive table of contents. In addition to the table of contents, the book contains an author index, which includes a complete list of sources (authors, standards, and Web sites), and a subject index, which allows the reader to select a topic to explore without having to go through the whole body of the text. Using these tools, those taking an open-book exam are sure to quickly find the right answer when asked, for example, about Likert's four management styles or Feigenbaum's eight stages of the industrial cycle.

A GUIDE TO SOURCE IDENTIFICATION

The source of each entry—whether it be a person, a standard, or a Web site—is indicated under the entry's title. Those who are interested may find full information about the source in the References at the end of the book. I can't help mentioning the fact that in some cases, in order to keep the structure of the book, we had to change the syntax of the authentic citation a bit, in no circumstances altering its original sense. In case the changes were significant, the phrase "adapted from" appears in front of the source.

There are cases when the source is identified as "Common knowledge," "Unknown," or "Constructed."

Let's clarify this classification.

Common Knowledge

Occasionally, as it happens, some things seem to be so evident, important, and known for so many years that nobody remembers their source, but keeps repeating them on each appropriate occasion. In these instances the term "common knowledge" was chosen.

Unknown

The "Unknown" label was selected for the anonymous entries whose contents are sure to belong to someone, but the author's name is either unknown or just has been neglected in the first place. I quite admit that real sources may exist, and those lapses are exclusively due to lack of knowledge at this moment, so any claims of authorship are most welcome and will be accepted with gratitude.

Constructed

Sometimes, while working on a paper, presentation, or report, and having read and "digested" a number of recommendations from different sources, I have compiled (constructed) my own insights. This creative process implies altering some known ideas and adding my own "recipes," recommendations, and observations. I do not consider these insights to be utterly my own creations, but I do not believe they are attributable to any other source either. That's how the label "constructed" emerged.

Acknowledgments

I would first like to express my appreciation to all the quality assurance experts who have been the inspiration for both my work and this book.

A book of this type, by its very nature, required the assistance of a great many people. I express my gratitude to all those who made a contribution.

My special thanks to my son, Max, and my daughter Anna, who supported me from the very beginning, as they always do.

I also owe a debt of gratitude to those who were so generous with their time and expertise, and whose comments were so enlightening: Atalia and Shlomo Ben-Meir, Olga Tzadikov, Rita Kaschavtzev, Chen Lutvak, Ronit Haan, Jacob Minidor, Zeev Reingold, Dr. Herb Hecht, Dr. Alex Barel, and Dr. Pavel Grabov. Each one contributed in his or her special way to my book.

Part One

Management and General Wisdom

There is nothing new under the sun.
—Ecclesiastes. 1:9–10

Nine-tenths of wisdom consists in being wise in time.
—Unknown

Knowledge can be communicated, but not wisdom. One can find it, be fortified by it, do wonders through it, but one cannot communicate and teach it.
—Hesse 1951

Do things right the first time
Common knowledge

This slogan is intended to motivate workers to raise their productivity by listening to internal and external customers, determining their requirements, and doing the best they can to meet those requirements the first time.

Remark. You never have a second chance to make a good first impression.

First things first
Adapted from Covey, Merrill, and Merrill 1994

The main thing is to keep the main thing the main thing. When planning, first define what the "main thing" is. For example, no matter how good the garden's design, if there's no gardener, there's no garden.

One of a kind
Adapted from Deming 1997

Everything is one of a kind. Every product should be regarded as one of a kind. A job shop is a producer of one of a kind, although the shop may make one or it may make two hundred of the same thing.

The question is this: Is every job in a job shop done better than the one before? (See also Deming's *Fourteen obligations of top management,* point 5.)

One rhetorical question for workaholics
Covey, Merrill, and Merrill 1994

How many people on their deathbed wish they'd spent more time at the office?

One versus one-half
Hesiod c. 700 B.C.

Fools, they do not even know how much more is the half than the whole.

Owning 1%
Mackay 1988

Owning 1% of something is worth more than managing 100% of anything.

The first real alternative to the "best"
Adapted from Covey, Merrill, and Merrill 1994

Decisions are easier when they are a question of "good or bad." But for most of us, the issue is not "good" versus "bad" but the "best" versus the "good." The enemy of the "best" is the "good". . .

The only way to know . . .
Lord Kelvin 1889

The only way to know is to measure.

Remark. This may sound good, but it raises the question, especially today in the era of computerized treatments and analyses, of whether the measurement is really adequate. By assigning numbers without really understanding the measurement, one may create problems rather than solve them. Thus, under certain circumstances, so-called process metrics or indicators can generate misunderstandings, provide false information, and even lead to faulty decision making.

The only way to succeed in establishing a quality system
Unknown

The only way to succeed in establishing a quality system is SDDS: "Say what you Do, and Do what you Say."

One-to-one exchange
Mackay 1988

When a person with money meets a person with experience, the person with the experience winds up with the money and the person with the money winds up with the experience.

 Remark. One good turn deserves another.

The first principle of systems thinking
Senge 1990

Structure influences behavior. When placed in the same system, people, however different, tend to produce similar results.

One message about living a meaningful life
Covey, Merrill, and Merrill 1994

A meaningful life is not a matter of speed or efficiency. It's much more a matter of what you do and why you do it than how fast you get it done.

Work it right
Joe E. Lewis, cited in Silber 1998

You only live once, but if you work it right, once is enough.

 Remark. Do it right the first time, especially if you only have one shot.

The first step in quality information system planning
Common knowledge

The first step in quality information system planning is the definition and analysis of the required output. To accomplish this, you should understand what your information needs are.

Single sourcing establishes a partnership
Denton and Boyd 1994

"Single sourcing" that leads to a partnership puts you on the road to success. In 1980, with 5000 suppliers and a shipment defect rate of 8 percent, Xerox moved to single sourcing, becoming the forerunner of the "vendor certification" program so popular in the 1990s. As a result, Xerox's cost of materials dropped by 50 percent and its overhead for material management dropped by two-thirds. An additional bonus was that the number of defects fell from 10–25 per thousand to an impressive 350 per million.

One megabyte only
Barel 1991

It doesn't matter how large your computer disk is; finally you'll have only one megabyte free.

Lateral thinking: one way the mind can work
De Bono 1990

The need for lateral thinking arises from the way the mind works. Though the information-handling system called the mind is highly effective, it has certain characteristic limitations. These limitations are inseparable from the advantages of the system since both arise directly from the nature of the system. It would be impossible to have the advantages without the disadvantages. Lateral thinking is an attempt to compensate for these disadvantages while one still enjoys the advantages.

Two types of personalities and progress
Bernard Shaw

1. The reasonable man adapts himself to the world

2. The unreasonable man persists in trying to adapt the world to himself

Therefore all progress depends on the unreasonable man.

The advantage of postulating over convincing
Bertrand Russell 1917

The method of postulating has many advantages. They are the same as the advantages of theft over honest toil.

Two Qs
Adapted from Juran and Gryna 1988

A "little q" versus a "Big Q": Solving specific product problems is a "little q" policy. Having teams throughout the company to solve all process, manufacturing, support, and business problems (for all customers who are affected, external and internal) would be a "Big Q" policy.

Two Cs
Cortada and Woods 1995

A "little c" versus a "Big C": This phrase differentiates between external customers ("Big C") and fellow employees (internal customers, or "little c"). The concept is useful in process improvement and reengineering. It reminds us that all people can be viewed as customers and that we should treat them with courtesy and give them the best-quality goods and services possible.

Two things necessary to inspire trust
Covey, Merrill, and Merrill 1994

Both character and competence are necessary to inspire trust.

1. Character includes:

   • Integrity

   • Maturity

   • An abundance mentality (one that can accommodate a large quantity of alternatives)

2. Competence includes:

   • Technical competence

   • Conceptual competence

   • Interdependent competence

Two heads are not always better than one
Adapted from Hammer and Champy 1994

A case manager serves as a buffer between a complex process and the customer, acting as if he or she were responsible for performing the entire process.

Two organizational goals and related information

Constructed

1. Strategic goals (related to organizationwide issues):

   • Company vision, mission statement, and quality policy

   • Noise factors (uncontrollable environmental factors)

   • Benchmarking information and other field intelligence on the competition

   • Strengths, weaknesses, opportunities, and threats (SWOT)

2. Tactical goals (derived from the strategic goals):

   • Inspections, tests, and surveys

   • Defects, scrap, rework, and defective rates

   • Vendors' and contractors' ratings, mailing, and supply

   • Marketing, customer requirements, and feedback

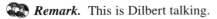

Two managerial alternatives and their corresponding results

Adams 1996

• Do nothing, and then get tired of doing nothing.

• Do irrational and unproductive things, and then get rewarded for being a can-do manager who makes things happen.

Remark. This is Dilbert talking.

Two factors that undermine the "80/20" rule of thumb
Raftery 1994

1. Method of measurement: For example, has the bill been prepared by measuring units of finished work in place or by measuring operations and taking time- and method-related charges as separate items?

2. Changes in technology: For example, in construction, the spread of costs over construction projects can change as a result of changes in design and construction methods.

Two kinds of customers
Hayslip 1994

	Quantity	Purchases	Knowledge about the Product
Consumer customer	A large number	Small in actual dollar amount	Not very knowledgeable
Business customer	A small number	Large in actual dollar amount	Knows more than the producer

Two major thrusts of enterprise
Atkinson, Hamburg, and Ittner 1994

1. Strategic quality planning
2. Quality-based cost management

Two basic strategies adopted by successful companies
Atkinson, Hamburg, and Ittner 1994

1. Offer superior value
2. Lower costs by using quality tools and techniques

Two types of Baldrige Criteria items
Malcolm Baldrige National Quality Award Web site

1. Approach/deployment: What the organization does to be a success

2. Results: What the organization achieves

Two types of European Quality Award Criteria items
EFQM Web site

1. Enablers: What the organization does to be a success

2. Results: What the organization achieves

Two top levels in supply chain management
Common knowledge

1. STS (ship-to-stock)

2. JIT (just-in-time)

Remark. Both levels are based on the replacement of inspection activities with audits. STS is often a predecessor of JIT procurement.

Two types of actions in quality improvement: reactive and proactive
Common knowledge

1. Corrective action: An action taken in reaction to an existing nonconformity or other undesirable event in order to reduce or eliminate its causes

2. Preventive action: A proactive action, usually consisting of a number of measures, taken to achieve quality and prevent the occurrence of a quality deficiency

Think fuzzy: multivalence versus bivalence
Adapted from Kosko 1993

Aristotle's binary logic (black and white) came down to one law: A or not-A. Either this or not this. The sky is blue or not blue. It can't be both blue and not blue. The Buddha lived in India five centuries before Jesus and almost two centuries before Aristotle. The first step in his belief system was to break through the black-and-white world of words, pierce the bivalent veil and see the world as it is, see it filled with "contradictions," with things and not-things, with roses that are both red and not-red, with A and not-A.

If our reasoning has logic, it's fuzzy at best. We have only one decision-making rule: *I'll do it if it feels right.*

The formal logic we first learn in tenth-grade geometry class has little to do with it. That's why we made it to tenth grade.

Fuzzy logic begins where Western logic ends.

Remark. The yin-yang symbol ☯ is the emblem of fuzziness.

Two types of improvement
Juran and Gryna 1988

1. *Project by project:* Ad hoc problem solving by a cross-functional quality improvement team from multiple departments of 4–8 members. Ideally, the project should deal with a chronic problem—one that has been awaiting a solution for a long time.

2. *By quality circle:* Problem solving within a department by establishing employee involvement groups of six to twelve members.

Two types of knowledge
Common knowledge

1. Explicit (open)

2. Implicit (tacit)

Dual responsibility within an organization

Source: *Project Management: A Systems Approach
to Planning, Scheduling, and Controlling,* 6th ed.,
by Harold Kerzner. Copyright 1998 by
John Wiley & Sons, Inc. Reprinted by permission
of John Wiley & Sons, Inc.

Subject	Line Manager	Project Manager
1. Direction	Summary	Detailed
2. Measurement/evaluation/control	Summary	Detailed
3. Rewards	Formal	Informal

Two types of leaders: project managers versus project champions

Source: *Project Management: A Systems Approach
to Planning, Scheduling, and Controlling,* 6th ed.,
by Harold Kerzner. Copyright 1998 by
John Wiley & Sons, Inc. Reprinted by permission
of John Wiley & Sons, Inc.

Aspect	Project Manager	Project Champion
Preference	Working in groups	Working individually
Commitment	To corporation To material values	To technology To intellectual values
Pursuit	To achieve what is possible	To achieve what is perfect
Thinking mode	Tactics	Strategy
Management	People	Things
Risk taking	Willing	Unwilling

Two kinds of language: judo-like and karate-like

Thompson and Jenkins 1993

1. *Verbal judo:* No weapons (see *First principle of judo,* p. 118)

2. *Verbal karate:* Sharp, quick blows (fighting, striking, kicking, attacking, offensive system)

Two prerequisites for use of "to be determined" (TBD)

1. A description of the conditions causing the "to be determined" (for example, why an answer is not known) so that the situation can be resolved

2. A description of what must be done to eliminate the "to be determined," who is responsible for its elimination, and by when it must be eliminated

---

Two types of traceability

1. *Backward traceability* (to previous stages of development): This depends upon each requirement's explicit referencing of its source in earlier documents.

2. *Forward traceability* (to all documents spawned by the software requirement specification): This depends upon each requirement in the SRS having a unique name or reference number.

Two basics of artificial intelligence
Common knowledge

1. *Declarative knowledge:* Facts

2. *Procedural knowledge:* Rules

Remark. Our brains are able to work "FIRO"—facts in, rules out.

Two complements to artificial intelligence
Unknown

1. Natural intelligence

2. Natural stupidity

Two versions of nominal grouping
Adapted from Mears 1995

1. Open version:
   - The facilitator presents the issue
   - The meeting begins with a period of silence
   - Members write their ideas
   - Ideas are presented round-robin fashion until the end
   - Ideas are clarified
   - Anonymous voting takes place

2. Anonymous version:
   - This version is used for sensitive issues
   - It encourages quiet or shy members
   - The facilitator presents the issue
   - Members anonymously write their ideas
   - Ideas are shuffled and written on the board
   - Ideas are clarified
   - Anonymous voting takes place

Two sets of rules for brainstorming
Adapted from Mears 1995

1. Conceptual rules:
   - Offer no criticism
   - Remain open-minded
   - Hitchhike on other ideas

2. Practical rules:
   - Speak in turn
   - Present one idea per turn
   - You may pass
   - Do not explain your ideas

Two facts about human nature
Adapted from Sinha 1993 and Leland and Bailey 1999

1. Dissatisfied customers tell an average of ten other people about their negative experience (in service business, up to twenty).

2. Satisfied customers tell an average of five other people about their positive experience (in service business, nine to twelve).

Two 50/50 families in the European Quality Award Criteria
EFQM Web site

1. Enablers (50%):

   - Leadership

   - People management

   - Policy and strategy

   - Resources

   - Processes

2. Results (50%):

   - People satisfaction

   - Customer satisfaction

   - Impact on society

   - Business results

Two aspects of establishing a capability maturity model (CMM)
SEI 1994

1. *Institutionalization:* Commitment, ability, measurement, and analysis

2. *Implementation:* Activities and results

Two faces of customers' knowledge
Oscar Wilde, cited in SEI 1997

Nowadays people know the cost of everything and the value of nothing

Two important states in benchmarking
Common knowledge

1. *"State of the practice":* Your baseline—where you are and what you are doing

2. *"State of the art":* Where your strongest competitor is and what it is doing

Two kinds of experienced people
Unknown

1. Some people speak from experience

2. Others—from experience—don't speak

Two things necessary for an organization's success
Wanner and Franceschi 1995

1. Survival

2. Growth

Juran's trilogy
Adapted from Juran 1989

The three managerial processes used in managing for quality are planning, control, and improvement.

1. Quality planning:
   - Determine who the customers are
   - Determine the needs of the customers
   - Develop product features that respond to customers' needs
   - Develop processes that are able to produce those product features
   - Transfer the resulting plans to the operating forces

2. Quality control:
   - Evaluate actual quality performance
   - Compare actual performance to quality goals
   - Act on the differences

3. Quality improvement:
   - Establish the infrastructure for improvement
   - Identify the specific needs—the improvement projects
   - For each project, establish a project team with clear responsibility for bringing the project to a successful conclusion
   - Provide the resources, motivation, and training needed by the teams to:
     - Diagnose the causes
     - Stimulate establishment of a remedy
     - Establish controls to hold the gains

Three areas of customer satisfaction
Kessler 1996

1. *Expected quality:* This provides only a base threshold of satisfaction. Customer satisfaction stops once the basic requirement is met.

2. *Desired quality:* This increases customer satisfaction as more features or benefits are added to a product or service.

3. *Excited quality:* This causes the level of satisfaction to go way up when products and services go beyond basic expectations.

Three parameters that define field services
Common knowledge

1. Promptness

2. Competence

3. Integrity

Three Ps for rewarding people
Common knowledge

1. Plaque on the wall

2. Pat on the back

3. Presentation to management

Remark. These are all good, but in business process improvement projects, a fourth P should be added—a pat on the wallet (Harrington, Esseling, and Nimwegen 1997).

Three phases of management by policy
Adapted from Collins and Huge 1993

1. Establish policy:

   - Evaluate inputs to policies (drivers and influencers)

   - Assess customer needs, business environment, long-term plans, internal issues, current performance, critical success factors, and regulatory requirements

   - Formulate policies

   - Prioritize policies

   - Establish corporate indicators

   - Develop draft targets

   - Publish policies, indicators, and draft targets

2. Deploy policy:

   - Conduct analysis

   - Ensure participation/buy-in through catchball (two-way communication that results in joint commitment and joint ownership)

   - Use effective project management (for example, integrate with local business plans)

3. Implement policy:

   - Involve the "management web" (CEO, objective leader, CEO's management team, cross-functional management team, and progress review team)

   - Include management by policy as well as daily management

Three types of management involvement definitions
Senge 1990

1. *Compliance "by law":* Follows the "letter of the law" of the vision and the mission.

2. *Enrollment:* Exercises free choice to follow the company vision and mission.

3. *Commitment:* Definitely wants the vision and the mission to come alive, and will do what is necessary to make it happen.

Three partnership styles
Adapted from Poirier and Houser 1993

1. *Alliances and strategic alliances:* These consist of the development of an association (partnership) with one or more companies. Alliances allow the partners to be bigger than their parts; to have more effect than they would on their own. The alliance should benefit all the involved parties.

2. *Partners:* These are joint parties in a common business or purpose. The parties are on the same team, with equal rights.

3. *Business partnering:* This is the creation of an alliance or partnership. There is a pooling of resources in a trusting environment focused on continuous, mutual improvement.

Three phases of the ship-to-stock program
Bossert 1988

The ship-to-stock program is the supplier selection, approval, and certification process that consists of:

- Candidacy

- Qualification

- Maintenance

Three types of design considerations
Adapted from Taguchi 1987

1. *System design* includes the selection of parts, methods, and tentative product parameter values

2. *Tolerance design* is the establishment of the permissible variation in the product and process that will achieve a consistent output

3. *Parameter design* is the selection of nominal product and process operating levels to determine the optimum combinations of the parameter's levels (values)

Three tests for a core competence
Prahalad and Hamel 1990

1. It provides potential access to a wide variety of markets

2. It makes a significant contribution to the perceived customer benefit of the product

3. It should be difficult for a competitor to imitate

Three stages of evolution according to Dilbert
Adams 1996

1. First, there were some *amoebas*

2. Deviant amoebas adapted better to the environment, thus becoming *monkeys*

3. Then came *total quality management*

Three lessons taught by the direct response group
Hammer and Champy 1994

1. Reengineering must be an iterative process

2. Make good use of pilots and proofs of concepts in order to reduce the risk of proposed changes

3. Pay attention to the company's human resource and organizational infrastructure

---

3D (Three-dimensional) vision of Norm Phelps of Direct Response Group
Hammer and Champy 1994

1. Caring

2. Listening

3. Satisfying . . . one by one

Three hints for gaining profits from your patent
Patentcafe Web site

1. Stop using the word *idea.* An idea is simply the 1 percent inspiration part of the business formula. Begin thinking about, and committing to, your *product.* Products *sell* and therefore can have value; ideas don't sell—that's why *ideas* are worth a dime a dozen (or less) to big business.

2. Think about a patent not as the goal, but merely as a protection to help ensure that the investment you make in your *product* is not wiped out by a larger company that would steal your technology.

3. Begin your planning process on how to bring your product to market—not on how to protect your idea. You can protect your idea with a simple phone call to your patent attorney—keep focused on building value in your *product.*

Three kinds of companies
that undertake reengineering
Adapted from Hammer and Champy 1994

1. Companies that find themselves in deep trouble

2. Companies that are not yet in trouble but whose management has the foresight to see trouble coming

3. Companies that are in peak condition

Three realities that are true
for any company
McCormack 1984

1. Survival of the fittest

2. Your peers are your natural allies

3. There is always a system

Three hard-to-say phrases
that are essential to success
McCormack 1984

1. I don't know

2. I need help

3. I was wrong

Three excuses to take a phone call
during a meeting
McCormack 1984

1. When you are training a subordinate and you want him or her to learn firsthand about the facts of a particular situation

2. When you decide that the call might be germane to the meeting at hand

3. When the person who is calling might favorably impress the person you are with

---

Three categories of project managers
Baker and Baker 1998

1. Those who watch what happens

2. Those who make things happen

3. Those who wonder what happened

Three major reasons for determining the cost of poor quality
Unknown

1. To get management's attention

2. To provide an objective measurement

3. To pinpoint areas where corrective action will be profitable and cost-effective

---

Three dimensions of business achievement
Bredrup and Bredrup 1995

1. *Result direct metrics:* Direct metrics for business achievement (what and when)

2. *Diagnostic indirect metrics:* Indirect metrics for business achievement (where and how)

3. *Competence metrics:* Capability of future business achievement (needs and requirements)

Three common approaches to increasing job satisfaction
Common knowledge

1. *Job rotation:* Having people rotate among different jobs on a formally organized basis

2. *Job enlargement:* Amalgamating a number of different tasks into a single job

3. *Job enrichment:* Changing the job itself to make it more interesting to the individual

---

Three hints on performing supervisory and managerial jobs more effectively
Kogan Page 1993

1. Use daily planning to concentrate on priorities

2. Organize paperwork and records effectively

3. Eliminate or reduce time-wasting activity

Three qualities of charismatic leaders
Unknown

1. They make reference to the achievements of the past

2. They postulate a vision of the future

3. They influence action in the present

Three key characteristics for the user
Unknown

1. Fit

2. Performance

3. Service life

Three parameters that define field services
Common knowledge

1. Promptness

2. Competence

3. Integrity

Three ingredients of effective time management
Constructed

1. Values

2. Priorities

3. Willingness to interrupt management

Three levels of performance
Constructed

1. *Organization:* Business needs

2. *Process:* Performance needs

3. *Job/performance:* Learning and work environment needs

Three Fs of system problems
Bluvband 2001

1. *Flaw:* A flaw is an attribute that makes something, like a product or an operator's work, imperfect. Other terms for a flaw include the following:

   • Error

   • Imperfection

   • Inaccuracy

- Mistake

- Blemish

- Deficiency

- Defect

- Boo-boo

Two consequences of a flaw are possible:

- System fault (without failure)

- System failure

2. *Fault:* A fault is an "activated" flaw, such as the use of the flawed component or the improper use of the correct component. Two consequences of a fault are possible:

- Proper operation result if the system can tolerate the fault

- System failure

3. *Failure:* Failure is an improper system operation result.

———•••———

Three-*mu* checklist of *kaizen* activities
Imai 1986

1. *Muda* (waste)

2. *Muri* (strain)

3. *Mura* (discrepancy)

Each one of the above three *mu*s encompasses a checklist that includes the following eleven issues:

- Manpower

- Technique

- Method

- Time

- Facilities

- Jigs and tools
- Materials
- Production volume
- Inventory
- Place
- Way of thinking

Three As of change management
Unknown

1. Adopt
2. Adapt
3. Advance

Three Ds of a well-established quality system
Bluvband 2001

1. Defined
2. Documented
3. Doable

Rule of three
Stone 2001

1. *For you:* Be pleasant, be trusting, be bold.
2. *For others:* Be uplifting, be positive, be enabling.
3. *For your principles:* Be controlling, be unreasonable, be clear.

Three types of product features
Kusiak 1993

Each of the needs expressed by customers corresponds to one of the three types of features:

1. *Basic features:* These are assumed but not stated

2. *One-dimensional features:* These are usually stated in specification; one-dimensional features increase customer satisfaction as their performance improves

3. *Excitement features:* These delight the customer and differentiate a product from its competitors

---

Three stages in context-free questioning
Gause and Weinberg 1989

1. Focus on the customer, the overall goals, and the benefits

2. Ask questions for better understanding

3. Focus on the effectiveness of the meeting

Aristotle's three basics for giving good talks
Aristotle, *Rhetoric,* fourth century B.C.

1. Have a central idea

2. Know your audience

3. Divide your talk into a beginning, middle, and end

Three historical examples that dispute the quality cost approach
Bluvband 1999a

Failure prevention is one of the core issues of the theory of quality in general and quality cost in particular. The common belief—the higher the investment in failure prevention, the bigger the economic gain—is not that obvious and has proved to be quite dubious throughout human history.

The City of Venice

Owing to the faults of the initial architectural project, the city of Venice has to cope with progressive sinking of the land and with the "high water" phenomenon. Despite this, or rather thanks to this, millions of tourists have come to Venice, bringing huge profit for the city. As James Morris said, "Nothing in the story of Venice is ordinary. She was born dangerously, lived grandly, and never abandoned her brazen individualism."

The Leaning Tower of Pisa

An outstanding example of Romanesque architecture, the tower in Pisa, Italy, started leaning during its fifth year of construction. The architect failed to foresee that the tower was built on unsuitable ground to sustain such a tall building. His failure resulted in the creation of one of the wonders of the world, bringing enormous tourist business to Pisa and providing livelihood to generations of architects and construction workers.

Columbus's Search for the Indies

Columbus took the wrong direction and applied the wrong motivation and conflict resolution techniques. He didn't plan quality training, calibrate the equipment, apply quality procedures, use the appropriate configuration control and incoming inspection, or employ the right teams. He used the wrong maps, got lost, and didn't get to the Indies, his initial destination. . . . But as a result, the new continent of America was discovered. No one nowadays doubts the profitability of his mistake.

Remark. It is in human nature to attempt again and again to correct even the most "profitable" mistakes: the $2.6 billion project to save Venice, which will take about eight years to complete, has been approved in Italy; the $30 million project to stabilize the 12th-century bell tower of Pisa was completed in 2001, making the 200-foot-high tower safe for the next 300 years; and since Columbus's discovery, unimaginable amounts of money have been invested in making America a better place.

No doubt new "profitable" mistakes will abound.

Four pointers on retaining your customers
Adapted from Furlong 1993

1. *Know who your best customers are.* The best customers are defined as those that benefit the company's profitability. The customer that buys the most may not be the best. Analysis may reveal that big customers lose big dollars. The actual and total costs to serve a customer must be considered. There are four key factors to look at:

   • Amount of support services needed

   • Special client production needs

   • Distribution via just-in-time

   • After-sale service and benefits

2. *Segment the best customers.* Develop a computer database to detail each customer's relationship with the company.

3. *Offer a price for profit.* Create ways to pay your best customers for using your services. (In most businesses 90 percent of the profit comes from 10 percent of the customers). Reward customers for frequency of stays or for the amount spent with the company.

4. *Consider a strategy to remove excess services from the lower-profit customers.* The most money is made at the higher end. The lower-echelon customers need not necessarily be given the same special benefits that the higher-echelon ones receive.

Deming's four elements of profound knowledge
Deming 1994

1. Appreciation for a system

2. Knowledge about variation

3. Theory of knowledge

4. Understanding of psychology

Four balanced scorecard perspectives
Adapted from Kaplan and Norton 1993

1. *Shareholders* (How should we appear to our shareholders?). Return on investment, cash flow, sales backlog.

2. *Processes* (What business processes must we excel at?). Rework, cycle time reductions, setup time reductions.

3. *Employees* (How will we sustain our ability to change and improve?). Employee surveys, $/employee, percentage spent on training.

4. *Customers* (How should we appear to our customers?). Customer surveys, complaints logged, market share.

Four rules of leadership and management styles
Hersey and Blanchard 1982

1. *Directive:* Telling and directing what to do

2. *Selling:* Coaching, helping the employee to learn, yet still directing his or her actions

3. *Participating:* Giving guidance to the employee, who is now skilled in his or her work

4. *Delegating:* Assigning responsibility to the employee, who is now skilled and willing to do the work at hand

Four phases of quality focus
Unknown

1. Formulation

2. Deployment

3. Implementation

4. Review

Four elements of the quality assurance model
Common knowledge

1. Testing

2. Inspection

3. Control

4. Audit

Four company strategy types
Bensley and Wortman 1995

1. *Leading edge* (first to market: concentration on technology stretch). Leading edge companies have the objective of being the first to produce and market new products ahead of everyone else. Their products are almost always high priced.

2. *Fast follower* (high quality, good price; concentration on value engineering). Fast follower companies market high-quality, reliable, reasonably priced products that are produced in high volume and marketed in an efficient manner.

3. *Commodity producer* (high volume, good price; concentration on value engineering). Commodity producers are companies that produce a high output at a low price.

4. *Trailing edge* (supply the need; concentration on quality control). Trailing edge companies make a living producing products that have gone through the three prior stages with only a low-volume market left to serve. They exist because they operate in a market in which others have no interest.

Likert's four management styles
ASQ's Foundations in Quality 1998

1. *Exploitative authoritative.* One-way communication flows only from manager to subordinate. Horizontal information transfer between peers is strongly discouraged. This is the purest form of autocratic, dictatorial management.

2. *Benevolent authoritative.* Downward communication prevails. Some upward communication from subordinate to manager exists, but only at the manager's discretion. Horizontal peer communication is discouraged.

3. *Consultative.* Open communication exists between managers and subordinates. Management actively seeks individuals' ideas and opinions. However, this style of open communication between subordinates is frowned upon.

4. *Participative.* Managers and subordinates communicate openly and freely. The manager is a leader, facilitator, and coordinator of a team effort. The group assumes responsibility and authority.

Four phases of implementation plans
Unknown

1. Start-up:

   • Educate management in concepts

   • Develop council procedures

2. Practicing of concepts by department managers:

   • Make formal proposals to council

   • Get recognition and award programs operational

3. Pilot department implementation:

   • Create self-control groups

   • Implement and revise council procedures

4. Scale-up across firm:

   • Concentrate on employee involvement

Four contemporary demands of quality
Hammer and Champy 1994

1. Service

2. Flexibility

3. Low cost

4. Simplicity of process

ASQ's four-part code of ethics
ASQ's Foundations in Quality Learning Series 2001

I acknowledge that I:

1. Fundamental principles:

   • Will be honest and impartial; will serve with devotion my employer, my clients, and the public.

   • Will strive to increase the competence and prestige of the profession.

   • Will use my knowledge and skill for the advancement of human welfare and in promoting the safety and reliability of products for public use.

   • Will earnestly endeavor to aid the work of the Society.

2. Relations with the public:

   • Will do whatever I can to promote the reliability and safety of all products that come within my jurisdiction.

   • Will endeavor to extend public knowledge of the work of the Society and its members that relates to the public welfare.

   • Will be dignified and modest in explaining my work and merit.

   • Will preface any public statements that I may issue by clearly indicating on whose behalf they are made.

3. Relations with employers and clients:

   • Will act in professional matters as a faithful agent or trustee for each employer or client.

- Will inform each client or employer of any business connections, interests, or affiliations that might influence my judgment or impair the equitable character of my services.

- Will indicate to my employer or client the adverse consequences to be expected if my professional judgment is overruled.

- Will not disclose information concerning the business affairs or technical processes of any present or former employer or client without his or her consent.

- Will not accept compensation from more than one party for the same service without the consent of all parties. If employed, I will engage in supplementary employment of consulting practice only with the consent of my employer.

4. Relations with peers:

- Will take care that credit for the work of others is given to those to whom it is due.

- Will endeavor to aid the professional development and advancement of those in my employ or under my supervision.

- Will not compete unfairly with others; will extend my friendship and confidence to all associates and those with whom I have business relations.

Four ritual declarations of the uniqueness of construction
Raftery 1994

1. Each project is different

2. There are special problems in construction

3. The future cannot be forecast

4. Construction is a high-risk business

Remark. You can substitute any other field of business for construction.

Four suicidal dressing mistakes men make
Molloy 1975

1. They let their wives or girlfriends choose their clothing

2. They let their favorite salesclerks choose their clothing

3. They let designers and "fashion consultants" choose their clothing

4. They let their backgrounds choose their clothing

Four factors of program performance (efficiency)
Arthur 1985

1. Execution time

2. Input/output utilization

3. Memory usage

4. Program readability and maintainability

Four critical steps to transform business into competitive gain
Adapted from Atkinson, Hamburg, and Ittner 1994

1. *Process:* Define the quality process that embraces the strategic vision

2. *Improvement:* Improve profitability and customer satisfaction

3. *Productivity:* Eliminate non-value-added activities

4. *Profitability:* Redeploy resources from non-value-added activities into value-added activities

Four basic principles of
total quality management
Smith 1993

1. Customer satisfaction

2. Plan–do–check–act (PDCA)

3. Management by fact (often referred to as "speaking with facts")

4. Respect for people

Four common characteristics of
sex and quality
Crosby 1980

1. Everyone is for it

2. Everyone feels they understand it

3. Everyone thinks execution is only a matter of following natural inclinations

4. Most people feel that all problems in these areas are caused by other people

---

Four words that indicate
requirement necessity
Common knowledge

- *Shall* and *must* usually identify a mandatory (essential) requirement

- *Should* and *may* usually identify an optional (conditional) requirement

Constantine's four paradigms
Constantine 1993

There are four project management and organization paradigms:

1. *Closed* (traditional authority hierarchy):

    • *Decision making:* Formal, top-down by position

    • *Problem:* Mindless overcontrol

2. *Random* (innovative independent initiatives):

    • *Decision making:* Informal, bottom-up by individual

    • *Problem:* Destructive competition

3. *Open* (adaptive collaborative processes):

    • *Decision making:* Negotiated, consensual, by group process

    • *Problem:* Endless processing

4. *Synchronous* (efficient harmonious alignment):

    • *Decision making:* Unnegotiated, predefined, implied by vision

    • *Problem:* Drifting deadness

Four rules for agreeing with requirements
Unknown

The requirements should be:

1. Feasible

2. Clearly and properly stated

3. Consistent with each other

4. Testable

Four principles of evaluating
what you are told
Karrass 1993

1. Never take anything for granted

2. Check everything

3. Put everything in its proper context

4. Draw a sharp line of demarcation between facts and the interpretation of facts

---

Four core values in effective management
Hardjono, ten Have, and ten Have 2000

1. Business process focus

2. Customer focus

3. People focus

4. Learning focus

Four major influences on
specification of requirements
Schenck 1994

1. User profiles

2. Work flow analysis

3. Organizational profiles

4. Opportunity appraisal

Two don'ts and two dos of strategic alliances
Adapted from Robert 1993

1. Don't form an alliance to correct a weakness (yours or your partner's)
2. Don't license critical proprietary technology
1. Have unique strengths
2. Form alliances around unique capabilities

Four reasons to perform measurements
Hines et al. 2000

1. What gets measured gets done
2. What gets measured is only what gets done
3. What gets measured gets managed
4. What gets measured improves

Four tips on writing a letter of demand
Kaner and Pels 1998

1. Lay out your case in a clear and organized way
2. State clearly what you are asking for
3. Show that you are a reasonable person
4. Make it clear that this is a letter of demand

Juran's five basic quality building blocks
Juran and Gryna 1980

1. *Structural or technological* (for example, clarity of a cable television picture)

2. *Sensory or psychological* (for example, beauty of surroundings, comfort, and recognition of regular customers)

3. *Time-oriented* (for example, repair time, reliability, and other "-ilities")

4. *Commercial or contractual* (for example, a guarantee of satisfactory service)

5. *Ethical* (for example, honesty of service shops, principled and courteous conduct of personnel, and truth in advertising)

Five supplier management process elements
Adapted from ASQ's Foundations in Quality
Learning Series 2001

1. Performance evaluation

2. Supplier auditing

3. Supplier selection

4. Supplier certification

5. Supplier partnering

Maslow's hierarchy of five needs
Adapted from ASQ's Foundations in Quality Learning Series 2001

1. *Basic needs:* To eat, sleep, and have shelter

2. *Safety:* To have economic and physical security

3. *Belonging:* To be accepted by family and friends

4. *Self-esteem:* To be held in high regard and have status

5. *Self-actualization:* To achieve one's best

Five definitions of quality work
Constructed

1. Is fit for use

2. Conforms to requirements

3. Meets customer expectations

4. Is done right the first time

5. Possesses a degree of excellence

Five stages that define the lifecycle of a customer
Lowenstein 1995

1. *Acquisition:* Converting a prospect to a customer; has a high cost

2. *Retention:* Keeping the customer; one-quarter of the cost to acquire

3. *Attrition:* Fading of customer enthusiasm as dissatisfaction creeps in

4. *Defection:* Losing the customer

5. *Reacquisition:* Regaining the customer, but at a high cost

Five qualities of customer-driven organizations
Adapted from Albrecht 1992

1. *Market and customer research:* Meet the need to understand the customer and perform audits to determine present levels of supply and demand

2. *Strategy formulation:* Direct the focus toward customer satisfaction

3. *Training:* Give proper training to everyone, from top to bottom

4. *Process improvement:* After training, send teams out to find and fix problems in the process

5. *Measurement and feedback:* Use a system of measures in order to determine a baseline, to measure progress, and to measure results

Five qualities of customer-driven organizations
Schaaf and Zemke 1989

1. *Listen to the customer:* Customer needs

2. *Define a service strategy:* Customer focus

3. *Set standards of performance:* Needed for measures and results

4. *Select and train employees:* The right employees and proper training are important

5. *Recognize and reward accomplishment:* Not enough of this is done in American industry

Juran's five types of customer needs
Juran 1992

1. *Stated needs:* What the customer says he or she wants (a car)

2. *Real needs:* What the customer really wants (transportation)

3. *Perceived needs:* What the customer thinks is desirable (a new car is better than a used car)

4. *Cultural needs:* The status of the product (a BMW)

5. *Unintended needs:* Use of the product in an unintended manner (a BMW used by the customer to haul concrete blocks)

Five objectives of customer research
Gale 1994

1. Determine what quality is

2. Find out what competitors are doing

3. Define quality performance measures for use

4. Identify factors to give a competitive edge

5. Identify urgent problems

———•———

Five clauses of the
ISO 9001:2000 requirements
ANSI/ISO/ASQ Q9001-2000

4   Quality management system

    4.1 General requirements

    4.2 Documentation requirements

5   Management responsibility

    5.1 Management commitment

    5.2 Customer focus

    5.3 Quality policy

    5.4 Planning

    5.5 Responsibility, authority and communication

    5.6 Management review

6   Resource management

    6.1 Provision of resources

    6.2 Human resources

    6.3 Infrastructure

    6.4 Work environment

7   Product realization

    7.1 Planning of product realization

    7.2 Customer-related processes

7.3 Design and development

7.4 Purchasing

7.5 Production and service provision

7.6 Control of monitoring and measuring devices

8 Measurement, analysis and improvement

8.1 General

8.2 Monitoring and measurement

8.3 Control of nonconforming product

8.4 Analysis of data

8.5 Improvement

Five steps from customer order to installation
Hammer and Champy 1994

1. Determine the customer's requirements

2. Translate them into internal product codes

3. Convey the coded information to the various plants and warehouses

4. Receive and assemble the components

5. Deliver and install the equipment

Five steps on the long road to a patent
PatentCafe Web site

1. Find out whether anyone has invented your idea before you. Use your Internet connection and learn how to read patents. When you find an idea that's almost the same as your own, convince yourself it's different.

2. Decide whether you really need a second car or whether you want your idea to become your life's work. If unsure, go ahead and protect it with a patent.

3. Get some business and technical training while you wait for your patent to be granted. You will have lots of time, so buy more than one book.

4. Following the granting of the patent, sell a share of the idea to everyone including friends, relatives, and associates, and be certain to offer a free share to anyone whose expertise you can't afford to purchase. Use the money to manufacture the idea yourself.

5. When you are ready to start manufacturing, attend major trade shows and brag like an idiot.

Five elements of successful competition
Mackay 1988

1. Marketing strategies

2. Position papers

3. Long-range plans

4. Niches, goals, and objectives

5. Knowledge

Five quality dimensions (or customer requirements) of support
Hayes 1991

1. *Availability of support:* The degree to which the customer can contact the provider

2. *Responsiveness of support:* The degree to which the provider reacts promptly to the customer

3. *Timeliness of support:* The degree to which the job is accomplished within the customer's stated time frame or the negotiated time frame

4. *Completeness of support:* The degree to which the total job is finished

5. *Pleasantness of support:* The degree to which the provider uses suitable professional behavior and manners while working with the customer

Five common features of key process area (KPA) practices
SEI 1994

1. Commitment to perform

2. Ability to perform

3. Activities performed

4. Measurement and analysis

5. Verifying implementation

Remark. Five capability maturity model (CMM) maturity levels have in total 18 KPAs [(0 ÷ 7) KPAs per level]. (See also part V, *Eighteen key process areas in the CMM*, p. 314.) There are five common features of the KPAs, and each KPA has key practices that range in number from one to more than twenty.

Five activities that constitute the IDEAL model
SEI 1994

1. Initiating

2. Diagnosing

3. Establishing

4. Acting

5. Leveraging

Remark. IDEAL is a variation of the plan–do–check–act (PDCA) model.

Five stages of quality evolution
ASQ's Foundations in Quality Learning Series 2001

1. *1200–1800:* Age of craftspeople and guilds

2. *1800–1900:* Product orientation and mass production

3. *1900–1945:* Process orientation

4. *1945–87:* Birth of total quality management and advent of quality standards

5. *1987–?:* ISO 9000, MBNQA, and other international standards

---

The five most popular Japanese quality words
Common knowledge

1. *Kanban* means "visible representation" or "card." The *kanban* system turns around an empty component case with slots.

2. *Poka-yoke* means "mistake-proofing."

3. *Hoshin kanri* means "management by policy." (*Hoshin* means "a plan, policy, or aim"; *kanri* means "management").

4. *Kaizen* means "improvement."

5. *Keiretsu* means "series" or "system"—a group of enterprises held together by various ties to their mutual benefit.

Five levels of inventiveness
Altshuller 1998

Level	Degree of Inventiveness	Percent of Solutions
1	Apparent solution	32%
2	Minor improvement	45%
3	Major improvement	18%
4	New concept	4%
5	Discovery	1%

Five decision-making styles
Driver, Brousseau, and Hunsaker 1993

1. *Decisive:* "Get things done now" rather than planning for five years (Lee Iacocca, H. Ross Perot, Harry Truman, and Ronald Reagan)

2. *Flexible:* Easygoing, personable, nonconfrontational, and jumps around from one unrelated topic to another (J. Paul Getty, Donald Trump, and Franklin D. Roosevelt)

3. *Hierarchic:* Best single conclusion, prone to long-range planning and complex data analysis, focus on quality and perfection (Howard Hughes, David Rockefeller, Henry Kissinger, Woodrow Wilson, and Richard Nixon)

4. *Integrative:* Maximal-information-seeking, as many solution alternatives as possible, consensus-seeking (Thomas Edison, and John F. Kennedy during the Cuban missile crisis)

5. *Systemic:* Combination of integrative and hierarchic styles, both multifocused and unifocused (television detective Colombo)

Five competitive forces
Porter 1979

1. The threat of new entrants

2. The power of customers

3. The power of suppliers

4. Substitute products and services

5. Industry rivalry

Five steps of the theory of constraints
Goldratt 1990

1. Identify the system's constraints

2. Decide how to exploit the system's constraints

3. Subordinate everything else to the above decision

4. Elevate the system's constraints

5. Go back to step one

Five-step psychological progression of organization for a persuasive speech
Nishiyama 2000

1. Attention

2. Need

3. Satisfaction

4. Visualization

5. Action

Five basic elements of strategic planning
ASQ's Foundations in Quality 1998

1. *Vision and mission.* Vision statements describe what the organization wants to be—what it hopes to achieve in measurable terms. Mission statements describe why an enterprise exists. They define an organization's scope of business. Some organizations develop separate vision and mission statements. Other organizations incorporate the vision into the mission statement. Vision and mission statements are often included in the annual reports of publicly held companies.

2. *Core beliefs and value statements.* Core beliefs and value statements describe facets of the organization such as its beliefs, values, assumptions, credos, philosophies, principles, and priorities. These statements are the basic beliefs that drive organizational behavior. Core beliefs and value statements are representative of the organization's personality and culture—or "the way we do things around here." Similar to vision and mission, core beliefs and value statements often appear in an organization's annual report.

3. *Strengths, weaknesses, opportunities, and threats (SWOT) analysis.* A SWOT analysis evaluates key internal strengths (such as financially

strong market, employees) and weaknesses (for example, young company with a high debt load) and external opportunities and threats. The analysis considers factors such as the industry and the organization's competitive position, as well as functional areas and management. Opportunities are identified and limitations acknowledged to provide information for reasonable goals (for example, competition, internal capabilities).

4. *Goals and objectives.* An organization sets specific goals and objectives to help fulfill its mission and give it direction and purpose over a long period of time.

5. *Tactics.* Once goals and objectives are defined, organizations create tactics, strategies, and processes that will help them arrive at their objectives. Organizations develop divisional business plans that set appropriate goals and support the organization's tactics.

Five reasons that people underestimate projects
Unknown

1. No or inadequate historical data

2. Lack of knowledge or experience

3. Radical technological change

4. Essential environmental change

5. Optimistic approach and desire to win

Five steps in the process of negotiating
Yeomans 1985

1. Planning and preparing

2. Bidding

3. Discussing and compromising

4. Agreeing

5. Setting the stage for the future

Six correlates of quality
Garvin 1988

1. Price

2. Advertising

3. Market share

4. Cost

5. Productivity

6. Profitability

Six thoughts on partnership
Bell 1994

1. *Generosity.* Things will even out in the end. We do not keep score. If a partner needs help, then help him or her. The partner may help you next time. Your customer has a flat tire near your store. You go help him fix the tire.

2. *Trust.* We must believe in each other's word. We want the arrangement to work. The legal stuff is not needed to keep agreements.

3. *Joint purpose.* We share a similar vision, purpose, or mission. You are in a jam for supplies and it is past closing time; the storeowner remains open to help you out.

4. *Candor and honesty.* We are truthful and authentic with each other. If something is very slightly wrong, you will gladly accept and remedy any problem. Complaints are needed to solve customer problems.

5. *Fairness.* We want to have a state of fairness and equality in the relationship. It is not always 50–50, but we strive for it.

6. *Comfort.* The partnership provides a sense of familiarity and ease (the same familiar look and friendly service to customers throughout the country).

———•·•———

Covey's six total quality principles
Covey 1991

1. Faith, hope, humanity

2. Work, industry, research, testing

3. Constancy, consistency, predictability

4. Continuous improvement and progression

5. Feedback based on measurements

6. Virtue and truth in human relations

———•·•———

Six factors in achieving poor quality
Unknown

1. Poor communication between:

   • Customer and producer

   • Contractor and producer

   • Engineering and manufacturing

2. Lack of communication between departments

3. Lack of feedback from the field

4. Poor (or no) training

5. Poor (or no) written procedures

6. Poor (or no) work instructions

Six factors in cooperating for quality
Unknown

1. Keep the doors of communication open

2. Place quality before quantity

3. Provide opportunities for improved employee relationships

4. Keep in mind that employees are capable of making creative contributions

5. Give employees authority

6. Train workers in advance for the future

Six points of postproduction quality service
Common knowledge

1. Warranties

2. Reliability

3. Customer complaint and failure analysis

4. Servicing of the product

5. Support tooling

6. Communication

Six Taylor versus six Deming management philosophy principles
Delavigne and Robertson 1994

The Taylor Method

- Professional management controls the business

- Management should make improvements happen through division of labor

- Management should control the variables of the system: workers, selection, motivation, training, supervision, and so on

- Management should develop systems to perform repetitive tasks

- Management should create the "one best way"

- Management should install a properly designed system to ensure that only outside influences can affect the system

The Deming Method

- Use leadership and cooperation

- Improvements occur through division of labor, use of creativity, and use of information

- Develop systems to perform repetitive tasks

- There is no one best way; variation constantly occurs in a system

- There is a need to understand the variation affecting a system

- Create a secure environment without fear in order to improve the system

---

Ishikawa's six requirements for making companywide quality control different
Ishikawa 1986

1. Institute more education and training in quality control

2. Maintain quality circles on a level equaling 20 percent of companywide quality control activities

3. Ensure participation by all members of the company

4. Implement quality control audits

5. Use the seven tools and advanced statistical methods

6. Promote nationwide quality control

Deming's six chain reaction elements
Deming 1997

1. Improve quality
2. Decrease costs
3. Improve productivity
4. Capture the market with better quality and price
5. Stay in business
6. Provide jobs

Six resources of project management
Source: *Project Management: A Systems Approach to Planning, Scheduling, and Controlling,* 6th ed., by Harold Kerzner. Copyright 1998 by John Wiley & Sons, Inc. Reprinted by permission of John Wiley & Sons, Inc.

1. Money
2. Manpower
3. Equipment
4. Facilities
5. Materials
6. Information/technology

Grabov's six versions of negative attitude toward consultants
Grabov 1998

1. If we have no problems, why do we need this guy (the consultant)?
2. Nothing could be improved here with our:
   - Managers (engineers, operators, . . .)
   - Technology (machines, tools, . . .)
   - Suppliers (subcontractors, customers, . . .)
   - Environment (everything)

3. This doesn't work in our situation. Our process is very complicated (special).

4. This guy (the consultant) has no relevant experience. We have been working here for 10 (20, 30, . . .) years and still do not know what to do. Are you serious with this consulting?

5. I have no time for this guy. Do you remember that we should work?

6. All consultants are liars (swindlers, . . .). You'll see in his report exactly what you tell him. We'll pay for nothing.

Six elements of the employee satisfaction survey
Heskett et al.1994

1. Job satisfaction

2. Training

3. Pay

4. Advancement fairness

5. Treatment: respect and dignity

6. Company's interest in employee well-being

Six elements of a world-class competitor
Watson 1993

1. Knows its processes better than its competitors know their processes

2. Knows the industry competitors better than its competitors know them

3. Knows its customers better than its competitors know their customers

4. Responds more rapidly to customer behavior than its competitors

5. Uses employees more effectively than its competitors

6. Competes for market share on a customer-by-customer basis

Six beliefs employees must hold
Hammer and Champy 1994

1. Customers pay all our salaries: I must do what it takes to please them

2. Every job in this company is essential and important: I do make a difference

3. Showing up is no accomplishment: I get paid for the value I create

4. The buck stops here: I must accept ownership of problems and get them solved

5. I belong to a team: we fail or we succeed together

6. Nobody knows what tomorrow holds: constant learning is part of my job

———•·•———

Six U.S. law-enforcement agencies helpful to a dissatisfied customer
Common knowledge

1. Federal Trade Commission

2. United States Postal Inspection Service

3. National Fraud Information Center

4. State attorney general

5. District attorney

6. Privately-funded agencies (for example, the Better Business Bureau)

———•·•———

Six issues that affect a manager's ability to achieve success
Arthur 1985

1. Managerial control costs

2. Unit costs

3. Cost proportions

4. Input prices

5. Output productivity

6. Input proportions

Six dos and six don'ts that successfully link quality to profits
Atkinson, Hamburg, and Ittner 1994

Do

1. Keep the assessment simple

2. Use the assessment to facilitate the improvement process

3. Measure all poor quality costs

4. Communicate the results

5. Consider setting reduction targets for the cost of poor quality

6. Encourage departmental and functional managers to be team members

Don't

1. Make the cost estimates too detailed

2. Exclude any department or function

3. Dollarize trivia

4. Make the assessment a witch-hunt

5. Use the cost of poor quality to compare departments

6. Create a new accounting system

Six levels of cognition
Blum 1992

1. Knowledge

2. Comprehension

3. Application

4. Analysis

5. Synthesis

6. Evaluation

Six new competencies
Scholtes 1998

1. Thinking in terms of systems and knowing how to lead systems

2. Understanding the variability of work in planning and problem solving

3. Understanding how we learn, develop, and improve; leading true learning and improvement

4. Understanding people and why they behave as they do

5. Understanding the interaction and interdependence between systems, variability, learning, and human behavior; knowing how each affects the others

6. Giving vision, meaning, direction, and focus to the organization

---

Six major components that are important to American customers
Denton and Boyd 1994

Americans rank the components of quality in the following order, according to a Yankelovich Clancy Shulman poll:

1. Reliability

2. Durability

3. Ease of maintenance

4. Ease of use

5. Brand name

6. Price

Six product lifecycle phases
(IEC Std. 60300-1, 2001)

1. Concept and definition

2. Design and development

3. Manufacturing

4. Installation

5. Operation and maintenance

6. Disposal

De Bono's six thinking hats
De Bono 1990

1. *White:* Facts, figures, and objective information

2. *Red:* Emotions and feelings

3. *Black:* Logical negative thoughts

4. *Yellow:* Positive constructive thoughts

5. *Green:* Creativity and new ideas

6. *Blue:* Control of the other hats and thinking steps

Seven deadly diseases that management must cure
Adapted from Deming 1997

1. Lack of constancy of purpose to plan products and services that will have a market and keep the company in business and provide jobs

2. Emphasis on short-term profits

3. Evaluation of performance, merit rating or annual review

4. Mobility of management; job-hopping

5. Use only of visible figures, with little or no consideration of figures that are unknown or unknowable

6. Excessive medical costs

7. Excessive costs of liability, swelled by lawyers that work on contingency fees

Luther's seven strategic planning process steps
Luther 1994

1. *Describe the vision of what the organization is to become.* Creating the vision is a key responsibility of senior management. A vision statement should make sense to everyone in the organization and should not require further explanation.

2. *List the premises that shape the organization and its capability of achieving its mission.*

3. *Develop the issues facing the organization on the basis of a premise list.*

4. *Develop the objectives that the organization should adopt.* Objectives address the real issues of the organization and not the petty problems. Properly developed, objectives are truly strategic in nature.

5. *Agree on how the objectives will be measured.* Measuring or defining results specifies the expected outcomes of the objectives.

6. *Select the strategies that will satisfy the objectives.* They should be sufficiently specific to enable formulating one-year plans. Each objective may have several strategies.

7. *Agree on a one-year plan and/or project plan.* The one-year plan and/or project plan define the task, when it is to be accomplished, and who should accomplish it.

Seven characteristics of productive meetings
Constructed

1. The reasons for the meeting and the outcomes sought are clear to participants in time for all material and ideas to be properly prepared.

2. Each item under consideration is discussed before being put on the agenda.

3. The meeting begins on time. Time limits are set and adhered to.

4. Attendance is limited to those people who are interested in the agenda and who are able to contribute to needed outcomes.

5. All materials, aids, and needed resources are gathered and set up in advance.

6. All participants are aware of everything that will be presented and discussed.

7. The participants keep the meeting program moving by proposing relevant plans, summarizing progress, understanding different views at appropriate points, and tactfully leading the discussion forward.

Seven off-line quality control aspects
Taguchi and Wu 1980

1. The quality of a manufactured product is measured by the total loss caused by the product to society

2. Cost reduction and continuous quality improvement are necessary to a healthy organization in a competitive economy

3. Quality improvement requires the never-ending reduction of variation in product and/or process performance around nominal values

4. Society's loss due to performance variation is frequently proportional to the square of the deviation of the performance characteristic from its nominal value (Taguchi loss function)

5. Product and process design can have a significant impact on a product's quality and cost

6. Performance variation can be reduced by exploiting the nonlinear effects between a product's or process's parameters and its desired performance characteristics

7. Product and/or process parameter settings that reduce performance variation can be identified with statistically designed experiments

Seven ways for the manager to avoid having paperwork pile up
Unknown

1. Take decisions immediately whenever possible. A memo or problem that goes into the "pending" file will have to be read and thought about again later.

2. Unless further information is needed, a decision will be no better for the delay, and there will be less time to put it right if it is wrong.

3. Make marginal notes on first reading when something cannot be dealt with immediately. This will save time later.

4. Reply by phone, when feasible, to save the time and expense involved in preparing letters, memos, and so on.

5. Discourage copies and written memos unless the supervisor or manager really needs to see them.

6. Ensure that reports submitted are actually used. Ascertain that there is no better way to disseminate information.

7. Set aside a regular, uninterrupted time for routine daily paperwork.

Seven taboos when making promises
Source: *Project Management: A Systems Approach to Planning, Scheduling, and Controlling,* 6th ed., by Harold Kerzner. Copyright 1998 by John Wiley & Sons, Inc. Reprinted by permission of John Wiley & Sons, Inc.

1. Promotion

2. Grade

3. Salary

4. Bonus

5. Overtime

6. Responsibility

7. Future work assignments

Seven-step plan for learning to read people
McCormack 1984

1. Listen aggressively

2. Observe aggressively

3. Talk less

4. Take a second look at first impressions

5. Take time to use what you've learned

6. Be discreet

7. Be detached

Seven types of management pitfalls
Source: *Project Management: A Systems Approach
to Planning, Scheduling, and Controlling,* 6th ed.,
by Harold Kerzner. Copyright 1998 by
John Wiley & Sons, Inc. Reprinted by permission
of John Wiley & Sons, Inc.

1. Lack of self-control (knowing oneself)
2. Activity traps
3. Managing versus doing
4. People versus task skills
5. Ineffective communications
6. Time management
7. Management bottlenecks

———•———

Seven reasons that people work
Scott and Jaffe 1991

1. Money
2. Promotion
3. Recognition
4. Job satisfaction
5. Job security
6. Meeting people
7. Achievement

———•———

The controllers' seven items that are the responsibilities of the administrative organization
Harrington, Esseling, and Nimwegen 1997

1. Business economic analysis and recommendations
2. Forecasts, estimates, and budgets

3. Calculations

4. Financing and credit review

5. Treasury

6. Taxes

7. Insurance

Seven benefits of customer loyalty
ASQ's Foundations in Quality 1998

1. *Lifetime value.* Loyal customers return again and again for more and more products and services.

2. *Increased purchases.* Loyal customers know the product line, trust the company, and are increasingly willing to buy more at any point in time.

3. *Referrals.* Loyal customers refer new business without the costs of marketing and advertising.

4. *Premium purchases.* Loyal customers are often less price sensitive.

5. *Employee retention.* Loyal customers contribute to job pride and satisfaction of employees, which in turn reduces costs of hiring and training and boosts productivity.

6. *Reduced operating costs.* Loyal customer accounts cost less to service because employees are more familiar with the customers' desires.

7. *Customer replacement cost.* It costs five times as much to gain a new customer as to keep an existing one and sixteen times as much to get a new customer to the same level of profitability as a loyal customer.

Seven themes in capability maturity models (CMMs)
SEI 1997

1. Continuous improvement

2. Defined, documented, and used processes

3. Commitment by senior management

4. Stable processes

5. Measured processes

6. Controlled processes

7. Evolving processes

Seven categories of quality definition
Constructed

1. Universal:

   - Quality is something that a person, thing, idea, and so on has which makes him, her, or it different, special, interesting, and so forth (McArthur 1981).

   - Quality is a special or distinguishing feature; the degree of goodness or worth (Hornby 1989).

   - Quality is neither mind nor matter, but a third entity independent of the two. . . . Quality cannot be defined, you know what it is (Pirsig 1974).

2. Manufacturing based:

   - Quality means conformance to requirements (Crosby1980).

   - Quality to the plant manager means to get numbers out and to meet specifications (Deming 1997).

3. User based:

   - Quality is fitness for use (Juran 1989).

   - Quality must be defined in terms of customer satisfaction (Deming 1997).

   - Quality is equivalent to customer satisfaction. The price of a product or service is an important part of its quality (Ishikawa 1985).

- Quality is the totality of characteristics of an entity that bear on its ability to satisfy stated and implied needs (ANSI/ISO/ASQC A8402-1994).

- Quality is the degree to which a set of inherent characteristics fulfills requirements (ANSI/ISO/ASQ Q9000-2000).

Remark. The "catch" is that in ISO 9000:2000 the term *requirement* does not have its typical meaning. Requirement is defined here as: "A stated need or expectation that is either implied or obligatory."

4. Product based:

- Quality refers to the amount of the unpriced attributes contained in each unit of the priced attribute (Leffler 1982).

5. Loss based:

- Quality is the loss a product causes to society after being shipped . . . other than any losses caused by its intrinsic function (Taguchi 1979).

6. Value based:

- Quality means best for certain customer conditions. These conditions are:

  - the actual use

  - the maturity

7. Multidimensional:

- Quality is multidimensional. It is virtually impossible to define the quality of a product or service in terms of a single characteristic or agent (Deming 1997).

- Eight dimensions of quality were identified in Garvin 1998 (see also *Eight Dimensions of Quality*).

  - Performance

  - Features Conformance

  - Reliability

  - Conformance

  - Durability

  - Serviceability

- Aesthetics
- Perceived quality
- Quality is a hierarchical multilevel complex of an object's attributes, properties, and characteristics intended to satisfy stated or implied needs (Bluvband 1995)

Seven rules of qualimetry
Adapted from Bluvband 1995

1. Create a quality breakdown structure (QBS)
2. Disjoint cost parameters from the functional parameters
3. Allocate the relative importance (RI) weights for each QBS item
4. Form an appropriate focus group
5. Brainstorm and define the quality rating (QR) chart for every basic quality element (BQE)
6. Determine the level of each BQE and the appropriate QR value
7. Integrate the values QR × RI bottom up

Remark. The term "qualimetry" was introduced first by Glichev et al. 1970.

Seven points for improving communication with internal customers
Lowenstein 1995

1. Company newsletters (basic information, corporate news)
2. Storyboards (a display on a specific company wallboard: memos, letters, project papers on subjects that would affect the employees)
3. Team meetings (an opportunity to share business news events)
4. Posting of customer letters of appreciation and dissatisfaction
5. Staff meetings
6. Displays of goals, progress charts, and so on
7. Quality awards from suppliers

Deming's eight chain reaction elements
Delavigne and Robertson 1994

1. Quality and productivity rise

2. Costs decrease

3. The time required for development and production is reduced

4. Management begins to know its cost: "it has a system"

5. Increased division of labor and specialization occur

6. The near-term future is more predictable

7. The standard of living rises

8 The system has a future and can provide "jobs and more jobs"

Eight management time fillers
Adams 1996

1. Renaming the department

2. Status reports

3. Teamwork exercises

4. Office relocations

5. Writing mission statements

6. Random organizational changes

7. Making view graphs

8. Micromanagement

Eight principle-centered characteristics of leaders
Covey 1991

1. They are continually learning

2. They are service oriented

3. They radiate positive energy

4. They believe in other people

5. They lead balanced lives

6. They see life as an adventure

7. They are synergetic (they improve things and situations)

8. They exercise self-renewal (physical, mental, spiritual, and emotional)

—·—

Eight crazymakers in the workplace
Scholtes 1998

1. Policies that force competition around a contrived scarcity

2. Policies of distrust and disloyalty

3. Dysfunctional systems combined with a culprit mentality

4. Paternalistic relationships

5. Narcissism, arrogance, and greed

6. Employees as objects of utility

7. Pathological loyalty: teamwork gone bad

8. "Lean and mean"-ism

Eight Fs: characteristics of people that cause failures
Weinberg 1993

1. *Frailty.* People, especially project managers, make mistakes. Accept it and prepare for it. In this way, people can catch each other's mistakes before they become too expensive to fix.

2. *Folly.* Someone did what they had intended, but the intention was wrong.

3. *Fatuousness.* Making the same mistake repeatedly without learning from it.

4. *Fun.* An attempt to make jokes.

5. *Fraud.* Illegally extracting personal gain from a project.

6. *Fanaticism.* Destroying something for revenge.

7. *Failure.* When programmers blame the hardware for software errors.

8. *Fate.* "Bad luck" (replace "luck" with "management").

———•·•———

Eight dimensions of quality
Adapted from Garvin 1988 and
Lindsay and Petrick 1997

1. *Performance.* The primary operating characteristics of a product.

2. *Features ("bells and whistles").* Those secondary characteristics that supplement the product's basic functioning.

3. *Reliability.* The probability of a product's functioning without failure within a specified period and under specified environmental conditions.

4. *Conformance.* The degree to which a product's design and operating characteristics meet preestablished standards, regulations, and laws.

5. *Durability.* The amount of use one gets from a product before it physically deteriorates.

6. *Serviceability.* The speed, courtesy, competence, and ease of repair.

7. *Aesthetics.* How a product looks, feels, sounds, tastes, and smells (subjective appraisal).

8. *Perceived quality.* An indirect measure that serves as the basis for comparing brands (usually inferred from various tangible and intangible aspects of the product: images, advertising, and brand names).

————•—•————

Eight EFQM basic concepts for an excellent organization
Europian Foundation for Quality
Management Web site

1. Customer focus

2. Supplier partnerships

3. People development and involvement

4. Processes and facts

5. Continuous improvement and innovation

6. Leadership and consistency of purpose

7. Public responsibility

8. Results orientation

————•—•————

Eight prerequisites for employees to perform efficiently
Source: *Project Management: A Systems Approach
to Planning, Scheduling, and Controlling,* 6th ed.,
by Harold Kerzner. Copyright 1998 by
John Wiley & Sons, Inc. Reprinted by permission
of John Wiley & Sons, Inc.

1. They must know what they are supposed to do, preferably in terms of an end product

2. They must have a clear understanding of authority and its limits

3. They must know what their relationship with other people is

4. They should know what constitutes a job well done in terms of specific results

5. They should know where and when they are falling short

6. They must be made aware of what can and should be done to correct unsatisfactory results

7. They must feel that their superior has an interest in them as individuals

8. They must feel that their superior believes in them and is anxious for their success and progress

---

Eight ISO 9000:2000 quality management principles
Adapted from ANSI/ISO/ASQ Q9000-2000

1. *Customer focus.* Emphasis on understanding their needs, meeting their requirements, and exceeding their expectations.

2. *Leadership.* Unity of purpose and direction of the organization; an internal environment in which people can become fully involved in achieving the organization's objectives.

3. *Involvement of people.* Use of their abilities for the organization's benefit.

4. *Process approach.* More efficient achievement of a desired result when activities and related resources are managed as a process.

5. *System approach to management.* Identification, understanding, and management of interrelated processes as a system—effectively and efficiently.

6. *Continual improvement.* Overall performance as a permanent objective of the organization.

7. *Factual approach to decision making.* Basing of effective decisions on the analysis of data and information.

8. *Mutually beneficial supplier relationships.* Interdependence of an organization and its suppliers; a mutually beneficial relationship that enhances the ability of both to create value.

Eight old rules and eight new rules relating to the organization of work
Adapted from Hammer and Champy 1994

1. *Old rule:* Information can appear in only one place at one time
   New rule: Information can appear simultaneously in as many places as it is needed

2. *Old rule:* Only experts can perform complex work
   New rule: A generalist can do the work of an expert

3. *Old rule:* Business must choose between centralization and decentralization
   New rule: Business can simultaneously reap the benefits of centralization and decentralization

4. *Old rule:* Managers make all the decisions
   New rule: Decision making is part of everyone's job

5. *Old rule:* Field personnel need offices where they can receive, store, retrieve, and transmit information
   New rule: Field personnel can send and receive information wherever they are

6. *Old rule:* The best contact with a potential buyer is personal contact
   New rule: The best contact with a potential buyer is effective contact

7. *Old rule:* You have to find out where things are
   New rule: Things tell you where they are

8. *Old rule:* Plans get revised periodically
   New rule: Plans get revised instantaneously

Eight ways to decrease productivity
Unknown

1. Careless management
2. Lack of goals
3. Wrong measurement
4. Lack of programs
5. Lack of training
6. Slowing down of capital investment
7. Societal changes
8. Lack of control

Eight things buyers dislike about a salesperson

Ehrlich and Hawes 1984

1. Overpromises and oversells

2. Misrepresents and exaggerates

3. Abuses telephone privileges

4. Talks prices in front of customers

5. Sells customers without buyer's consent

6. Carries stories about other people in the business

7. Tries to bribe prospects

8. Interrupts when buyer is busy

Nine time robbers

Source: *Project Management: A Systems Approach to Planning, Scheduling, and Controlling,* 6th ed., by Harold Kerzner. Copyright 1998 by John Wiley & Sons, Inc. Reprinted by permission of John Wiley & Sons, Inc.

1. Incomplete work

2. A job poorly done that must be done over

3. Delayed decisions

4. Poor communication channels

5. Uncontrolled telephone calls

6. Casual visitors

7. Waiting for people

8. Failure to delegate

9. Poor retrieval system

Nine European Quality Award Model elements
EFQM Web site

1. Leadership (10%)

2. People management (9%)

3. Policy and strategy (8%)

4. Resources (9%)

5. Processes (14%)

6. People satisfaction (9%)

7. Customer satisfaction (20%)

8. Impact on society (6%)

9. Business results (15%)

Nine waste categories: problems and solutions
Imai 1986

1. Work-in-process
   Problem: Stocking items not immediately needed
   Solution: Inventory improvement

2. Rejection
   Problem: Producing defective products
   Solution: Fewer rejects

3. Facilities
   Problem: Having idle machinery and breakdowns, taking too long for setup
   Solution: Increase in capacity utilization ratio

4. Expenses
   Problem: Overinvesting for required output
   Solution: Curtailment of expenses

5. Indirect labor
   Problem: Excess personnel due to bad indirect labor system
   Solution: Efficient job assignment

6. Design
   Problem: Producing products with more functions than necessary
   Solution: Cost reduction

7. Talent
   Problem: Employing people for jobs that can be mechanized or assigned to less-skilled people
   Solution: Labor saving or labor maximization

8. Motion
   Problem: Not working according to work standard
   Solution: Improvement of work standard

9. New-product run-up
   Problem: Making a slow start in stabilizing the production of a new product
   Solution: Faster shift to full line production

The nine biggest mistakes people make when seeking a job
Walton 1999

1. Not taking an active part in the job search

2. Not preparing for interviews

3. Relying on mass mailers as the primary job search technique

4. Believing that getting a great job is a matter of being in the right place at the right time

5. Overlooking the importance of being interesting

6. Believing grades are everything

7. Believing on-campus interviews are the only game in town

8. Believing that the first job determines the whole career

9. Believing that the best person gets the job

Nine principles of the benchmarking code of conduct (international benchmarking code)
Watson 1993

1. *Principle of legality.* If there is any potential question on the legality of an activity, don't do it.

2. *Principle of exchange.* Provide the same type and level of information that you request from your benchmarking partner to him or her.

3. *Principle of confidentiality.* Keep benchmarking interchange confidential to the individuals and companies involved.

4. *Principle of use.* Use information obtained through benchmarking only for purposes of formulating improvement.

5. *Principle of first-party contact.* Initiate benchmarking contacts, whenever possible, through a benchmarking contact designated by the partner company.

6. *Principle of third-party contact.* Obtain an individual's permission before providing his or her name in response to a contract request.

7. *Principle of preparation.* Make the most of your benchmarking partner's time by being fully prepared for each exchange.

8. *Principle of completion.* Complete each benchmarking study to the satisfaction of all benchmarking partners as mutually agreed.

9. *Principle of understanding and action.* Understand how your benchmarking partners would like to be treated.

Ten natural laws of successful time and life management
Smith 1994

1. You control your life by controlling your time

2. Your governing values are the foundation of personal fulfillment

3. When your daily activities reflect your governing values, you experience inner peace

4. To reach any significant goal, you must leave your comfort zone

5. Daily planning leverages time through increased focus

6. Your behavior is a reflection of what you truly believe

7. You satisfy needs when your beliefs are in line with reality

8. Negative behaviors are overcome by changing incorrect beliefs

9. Your self-esteem must ultimately come from within

10. Give more and you'll have more

Ten warning signs of fraud to watch for when dealing with invention promotion firms
Gibbs Group Web site

1. Nobody has more interest in your product idea than you do, so if you smell a rat terminate contact.

2. If you can't deal with the number-one person in charge, don't deal. There is *no reason* that you should not be working directly with a patent attorney or agent—instead of their salesman or secretary.

3. Make sure you get references from at least six inventors—don't accept the "our client information is confidential" answer.

4. If there is a single rumor of wrongdoing by the firm that you can verify—don't deal.

5. If they want the money up front for undefined or unmonitored services—don't deal.

6. They sign *your* confidential disclosure agreement or a negotiated version of it—or don't deal.

7. If they want significantly more payment than two weeks' services, regardless of the reasons or justification—don't deal.

8. Never pay for the services with a credit card number unless you can verify *everything* you need to know about the company.

9. Deal *only* with the person doing your work.

10. Only use specialists—don't deal with supermarket "we can do everything" service providers.

The ten biggest resume don'ts
Adapted from Walton 1999

1. Don't be too general

2. Don't drone on and on and on

3. Don't leave gaps in your chronology

4. Don't forget to proofread—and have other people proofread

5. Don't lie and don't mislead

6. Don't be cute

7. Don't leave valuable things off your resume by failing to appreciate the transferable skills they infer

8. Don't include personal information that hurts you

9. Don't use avant-garde visuals to get attention

10. Don't obsess over minutiae

Ten character traits of resource personnel and team leaders
Reliability Analysis Center 1992

1. Participative

2. Self-confident

3. Effective at dealing with people

4. Good at communicating

5. Trustworthy

6. Willing to take risks

7. Motivated

8. Visionary

9. Good at utilizing available resources

10. Able to explain statistics

Ten managerial roles
Mintzberg 1990

1. Figurehead

2. Leader

3. Liaison

4. Monitor

5. Disseminator

6. Spokesperson

7. Entrepreneur

8. Disturbance handler

9. Resource allocator

10. Negotiator

Ten things buyers like about a salesperson
Ehrlich and Hawes 1984

1. Respects buyer's time

2. Talks about "us" instead of his or her company—showing that he or she feels a part of it

3. Tells how product serves buyer's needs

4. Knows the products

5. Helps train buyer's employees in use of products

6. Makes appointments for sales calls

7. Lives up to promises

8. Doesn't inventory buyer's needs without a consent

9. Is courteous and neat in appearance

10. Pronounces buyer's name and company name correctly

Eleven attributes of a good manager
Adapted from Salisbury 1994

1. Behaves positively

2. Shows mutual respect

3. Enables instead of controls

4. Gives feedback

5. Appreciates a job well done

6. Leads by example

7. Makes people feel valued

8. Acts as a decision maker

9. Considers self a learner, not a teacher

10. Is available

11. Remains visible

Eleven controllable classifications of cost
Juran 1995

1. Waiting time

2. Employee activities

3. Training

4. Overtime

5. Setup and adjustment

6. Small tools and gauges

7. Repairs and maintenance

8. Salvage labor

9. Scrap

10. Supplies

11. Direct administration

Eleven things you should never say
Thompson and Jenkins 1993

1. Come here.

2. You wouldn't understand.

3. Because those are the rules.

4. It's none of your business.

5. What do you want me to do about it?

6. Calm down.

7. What is your problem?

8. You never . . . *or* You always . . . .

9. I am not going to say that again.

10. I'm doing that for your own good.

11. Why can't you be reasonable?

Eleven laws of systems thinking
Senge 1990

1. Today's problems come from yesterday's "solutions."

2. The harder you push, the harder the system pushes back.

3. Behavior grows better before it grows worse.

4. The easy way out usually leads back in.

5. The cure can be worse than the disease.

6. Faster is slower.

7. Cause and effect are not closely related in time and space.

8. Small changes can produce big results—but the areas of highest leverage are least obvious.

9. You can have your cake and eat it too—but not at once.

10. Dividing an elephant in half does not produce two small elephants.

11. There is no blame. You and the cause of your problems are part of a single system.

Eleven time wasters
Harris and Harris 1985

1. Things

2. Confusion

3. Inability to say no

4. Not knowing how to interrupt

5. Dulling sensation

6. Use of prime time for second-rate tasks

7. Television

8. Untimeliness

9. A perfectly clean house

10. Worrying about aging

11. Staying up late

Feigenbaum's twelve quality planning questions
Feigenbaum 1983

1. What specific quality work needs to be done?

2. When does each work activity need to be done during the product development, production, and service cycle?

3. How should the work be done: by what method, procedure, or device?

4. Who does the work and what is his or her position in the organizational chart?

5. Where is the work to be carried out and at what location in the plant: on the assembly line, in the laboratory, by the vendor, or in the field?

6. What tools and equipment are to be used?

7. What are the inputs to the work? What is needed in the way of information and material inputs to get the work done?

8. What are the outputs? Do any decisions have to be made? What are they, and what criteria should be used for making them? Does any material have to be identified and routed?

9. Is any record of the action to be made? If so, what is the form of the data? Is computer data processing required? What kind of analysis is required? To whom is it to be sent? What form of feedback is to be used?

10. Are there alternative courses of action to be taken that depend upon certain differences in the product quality encountered?

11. What are the criteria for these courses of action?

12. Is any time limit imposed on the work? If so, what is it?

———•·•———

Mackay's twelve Ps of competitive people
Mackay 1988

1. Pedigree

2. Physical scale

3. Performance as an investment

4. Pricing

5. People

6. Positioning

7. Plans

8. Performance as a supplier

9. Prestige in the business community

10. Probing for data

11. Prize fight . . . them versus us

12. Postmortem (examination of what could have been done)

Twelve improvement projects
Atkinson, Hamburg, and Ittner 1994

1. Improve product efficiency

2. Reduce fixed costs

3. Reduce direct materials costs

4. Reduce finished parts costs

5. Reduce engineering costs

6. Achieve price increase

7. Reduce raw material holding time

8. Increase manufacturing volume

9. Increase engineering service technology transfer sales

10. Reduce engineering development cycle time

11. Reduce premanufacturing engineering cycle time

12. Reduce manufacturing engineering cycle time

Twelve irrational beliefs about success
LeBoeuf 1979

1. The more you sweat, the more you get

2. Activity means productivity

3. Efficiency means effectiveness

4. Burn the midnight oil

5. The best way to get a job done is to do it yourself

6. The easy way is the best way

7. Hard work is virtuous

8. Work is not fun

9. There is only one best way

10. More discipline means less freedom

11. Justice for all

12. We work best under pressure

Feigenbaum's thirteen tasks for effective quality systems management
Feigenbaum 1983

1. Provide overall management of all activities of the quality system

2. Create, coordinate, and distribute quality-motivation programs

3. Establish performance standards and evaluation of overall quality progress in the area of key systems measurement

4. Review the effectiveness of corrective action programs

5. Resolve any intersystem incompatibilities that cannot be concluded by the personnel immediately involved

6. Ensure effectiveness of the system-audit program and the quality information feedback

7. Provide the focus of management attention to the activities of the quality system, ensuring their effective application toward achieving a common objective

8. Provide or obtain priority decisions for quality system activities when they compete with other programs for resources

9. Provide intracorporate liaison on the quality system

10. Ensure that the quality system is revised as required

11. Ensure the continuing effectiveness and business contribution of the quality-cost program

12. Provide leadership to ensure the effective use of the quality system as a specific factor in the company's business strategy

13. Ensure, as appropriate, the effective visibility of the quality system to customers and other relevant groups

---

Thirteen tips to get people to return your calls
Shook and Yaverbaum 1996

1. Have a positive attitude

2. Always be courteous to the secretary

3. Keep your answers brief

4. Understand the job of the secretary

5. Call early

6. Start and end your voice-mail message with your name and phone number

7. Respect your prospect's schedule

8. Be persistent

9. Be sure to talk to the decision maker

10. Create a sense of urgency with the secretary, but indirectly

11. Recruit secretaries as your allies

12. Use a third party as an introduction

13. Don't be discouraged if a phone call is not returned

Deming's fourteen obligations of top management
Deming 1997

1. Create constancy of purpose toward improvement of product and service

2. Adopt a new philosophy; we are in a new economic age

3. Cease dependence upon inspection as a way to achieve quality

4. End the practice of awarding business based on the price tag

5. Improve constantly and forever the system of production and service, to improve quality and productivity, and thus constantly decrease costs

6. Institute training on the job

7. Institute leadership

8. Drive out fear

9. Break down barriers between departments

10. Eliminate slogans/targets asking for zero defects and increased productivity without providing methods

11. Eliminate management by objective, management by numerical quotas

12. Remove barriers that stand between workers and their pride of workmanship

13. Institute programs for education and self-improvement

14. Put all emphasis in the company to work to accomplish the transformation

Fourteen top reasons that total quality management (TQM) initiatives fail
Unknown

1. Fragmented, partial approaches lead to "empowerment" without a clear strategy, which is chaos

2. Because of poor communication, few people really understand the program

3. Training is not tied to real problems, so there is no action learning

4. The TQM effort has an internal focus instead of being aimed at the customer

5. The focus is on cleaning up messes rather than on delivering superior product and customer service

6. A rigid, predetermined TQM program is imposed on the organization

7. The focus is on the company's performance instead of on how customers view its performance versus that of the competitors

8. Market research neglects key determinants of customer satisfaction or isn't adequately analyzed or communicated

9. The TQM effect is not aligned with the whole targeted market

10. The company adopts a customer value slogan but doesn't carefully develop competitive metrics

11. The TQM efforts are not connected to competitive strategy or business results

12. Segments within the targeted market are not clearly understood

13. Customers won and lost are poorly analyzed, so key market-driving factors are poorly understood

14. Inadequate quality effort is put toward innovation and cycle time

Dr. Kerzner's sixteen steps to project management maturity

Source: *Project Management: A Systems Approach to Planning, Scheduling, and Controlling,* 6th ed., by Harold Kerzner. Copyright 1998 by John Wiley & Sons, Inc. Reprinted by permission of John Wiley & Sons, Inc.

1. Adopt a project management methodology and use it consistently

2. Implement a philosophy that drives the company toward project management maturity and communicate it to everyone

3. Commit to developing effective plans at the beginning of each project

4. Minimize scope changes by committing to realistic objectives

5. Recognize that cost and schedule management are inseparable

6. Select the right person as the project manager

7. Provide executives with project sponsor information, not project management information

8. Strengthen the involvement and support of line management

9. Focus on deliverables rather than resources

10. Cultivate effective communication, cooperation, and trust to achieve rapid project management maturity

11. Share recognition for project success with the entire project team and line management

12. Eliminate nonproductive meetings

13. Focus on identifying and solving problems early, quickly, and cost-effectively

14. Measure progress periodically

15. Use project management software as a tool—not as a substitute for effective planning or interpersonal skills

16. Institute an all-employee training program with periodic updates based upon documented lessons learned

Seventeen Ms: fundamental factors that affect quality

Constructed

1. Market

2. Motivation

3. Money

4. Management

5. Men and women (personnel)

6. Materials

7. Machines

8. Modern information systems

9. Mounting product requirements

10. Merit

11. Mutuality

12. Major processes

13. Messages and communications

14. Methodology

15. Metrology

16. Maturity

17. Milieu

twenty-two

Twenty-two keys to creating a meaningful workplace
Terez 2000

Mission Keys

1. Purpose

2. Direction

3. Relevance

4. Validation

People Keys

5. Respect

6. Equality

7. Informality

8. Flexibility

9. Ownership

Development Keys

10. Challenge

11. Invention

12. Support

13. Personal development

Community Keys

14. Dialogue

15. Relationship building

16. Service

17. Acknowledgment

18. Oneness

"Me" Keys

19. Self-identity

20. Fit

21. Balance

22. Worth

Catch-22 situation of a quality manager
Bluvband 1998

You are the *adviser,* the *tester,* and the *slanderer,* and despite this *you still want people* to *pay you* for that and to *love you.*

twenty-seven

Twenty-seven organizing propositions
Adapted from Peters 1992

1. Most value added will come from headwork

2. Most work will be headwork

3. All former functional activities must be erased and turned into seamless wholes

4. Middle management layers destroy value

5. Most of tomorrow's work will be done in project teams

6. Project teams will enhance individual contributions

7. Learning multiple jobs and understanding the entire function of the team—and its relation to the enterprise—will be imperative

8. All work will encompass the major "functional" disciplines

9. Teammates have to depend upon each other

10. Trust is essential

11. The goal is more than "winning this game"

12. Dynamic, short-lived project configurations will be commonplace

13. The average project team will have at least a 75 percent chance of including outsiders

14. Who reports to whom will change over time, but accountability for a goal will be far higher

15. People will work more beyond functional walls

16. Feedback loops will be short

17. "Not letting down the side" is the principal motivation for the project team

18 New evaluation schemes are critical

19. There will be constant reorganization

20. Much of the value added will come from special learning, teaching, and communication devices

21. Organizational learning will be highly rewarded

22. Applying the new technologies to outmoded organizations is a design for disaster

23. Real-time access to all information is a must for everyone in the organization

24. The project manager and network manager are the players of tomorrow

25. The impermanent network will be used to execute almost every major task

26. (a) Systems integrators, (b) specialists, and (c) independent talents will be three principal sorts of "firms"

27. Marketplace power—not the amount of resources owned outright—will be critical

Augustine's fifty-two laws
Augustine 1987

Remark. Sixteen of the fifty-two fascinating Augustine's Laws are presented here. The roman numerals are the laws' original numbers.

1. If you can afford to advertise, you don't need to. (IV)

2. Decreased business base increases overhead. So does increased business base. (VII)

3. Bulls do not win bullfights; people do. People do not win people fights; lawyers do. (X)

4. It costs a lot to build bad products. (XII)

5. The last 10 percent of performance generates one-third of the cost and two-thirds of the problems. (XV)

6. It's easy to get a loan unless you need it. (XXI)

7. If stock market experts were so expert, they would be buying stock, not selling advice. (XXII)

8. Any task can be completed in only one-third more time than is currently estimated. (XXIII)

9. It is better to be the reorganizer than the reorganizee. (XXVIII)

10. The optimum committee has no members. (XXXI)

11. Ninety percent of the time things will turn out worse than you expect. The other 10 percent of the time you had no right to expect so much. (XXXVII)

12. The early bird gets the worm. The early worm . . . gets eaten. (XXXVIII)

13. Simple systems are not feasible because they require infinite testing. (XLII)

14. One should expect that the expected can be prevented, but the unexpected should have been expected. (XLIV)

15. A billion saved is a billion earned. (XLVI)

16. Regulations grow at the same rate as weeds. (XLIX)

One-hundred rules for NASA project managers
Project Management Body of Knowledge Web site

Remark. The introduction to this material at the Web site reads, "Jerry Madden, Associate Director of the Flight Projects Directorate at NASA's Goddard Space Flight Center, collected these gems of wisdom over a number of years from various unidentifiable sources. Rod Stewart of Mobile Data Services in Huntsville, Alabama, edited and updated them. The original link seems to have disappeared, so the entire list is included here to make sure that it remains available. If you know about or find any authoritative updates to this list, please send a message to the webmaster." Fifty of the one hundred rules for NASA project managers are presented here.

The Project Manager

- *Rule 1:* The project manager should visit everyone who is building anything for his or her project.

- *Rule 2:* The project manager must know what motivates the project contractors.

- *Rule 3:* The project manager finds the right people to do the work and gets out of the way so they can do it.

- *Rule 4:* Whoever the project manager deals with, he or she should deal with fairly.

- *Rule 5:* Vicious, despicable, or thoroughly disliked persons, gentlemen, and ladies can be project managers. Lost souls, procrastinators, and wishy-washies cannot.

- *Rule 6:* A comfortable project manager is one waiting for his or her next assignment or one on the verge of failure. Security is not normal to project management.

- *Rule 7:* One problem new managers face is that everyone wants to solve their problems. Old managers were told by senior management, "Solve your own darn problems, that is what we hired you to do."

- *Rule 10:* Not all successful managers are competent and not all failed managers are incompetent. Luck still plays a part in success or failure, but luck favors the competent hardworking manager.

- *Rule 13:* A manager who is his or her own systems engineer or financial manager is one who will probably try to do open-heart surgery on him or herself.

Initial Work

- *Rule 15:* Initial planning is the most vital part of a project. The review of most failed projects or project problems indicates that the disasters were well planned to happen from the start.

Communications

- *Rule 17:* Talk is not cheap, but the best way to understand a personnel or technical problem is to talk to the right people. Lack of talk at the right levels is deadly.

- *Rule 18:* Most international meetings are held in English. This is a foreign language to most participants such as Americans, Germans, Italians, and so forth.

People

- *Rule 20:* You cannot watch everything. What you can watch is the people. They have to know you will not accept a poor job.

- *Rule 21:* "Are old managers right or just old?"

- *Rule 23:* The source of most problems is people.

- *Rule 24:* One must pay close attention to workaholics—if they get going in the wrong direction, they can do a lot of damage in a short time.

- *Rule 26:* If you have someone who doesn't look, ask, and analyze, ask them to transfer.

Reviews and Reports

- *Rule 36:* Hide nothing from the reviewers. Their reputation and yours is on the line. Expose all the warts and pimples. Don't offer excuses—just state facts.

- *Rule 39:* The review is a failure if those reviewed learn nothing from it.

- *Rule 41:* Keeping the data simple and clear never insults anyone's intelligence.

- *Rule 42:* Managers who rely only on paperwork to do the reporting of activities are known as failures.

- *Rule 46:* Remember, it is often easier to do foolish paperwork than to fight the need for it. Fight only if it is a global issue, which will save much future work.

Contractors and Contracting

- *Rule 47:* Contractors don't fail, NASA does, and that is why one must be proactive in support.

- *Rule 48:* The project management measurement system should be used.

- *Rule 50:* Being friendly with a contractor is fine—being a friend of a contractor is dangerous to your objectivity.

- *Rule 53:* The ground rule is this: Never change a contractor's plans unless they are flawed or too costly (remember the old saying that better is the enemy of good).

Engineers and Scientists

- *Rule 55:* Overengineering is common. Engineers like puzzles and mazes. Try to make them keep their designs simple.

- *Rule 56:* The first sign of trouble comes from the schedule or the cost curve. Engineers are the last to know they are in trouble. Engineers are born optimists.

- *Rule 59:* Most scientists are rational unless you endanger their chance to do their experiment.

Hardware

- *Rule 61:* Most equipment works as built, not as the designer planned. This is due to the layout of the design, poor understanding on the designer's part, or poor understanding of component specifications.

Computers and Software

- *Rule 62:* Not using modern techniques, like computer systems, is a great mistake, but forgetting that the computer simulates thinking is a still greater mistake.

Senior Management, Program Offices, and Above

- *Rule 66:* Don't assume you know why senior management has done something. If you feel you need to know, ask. You get some amazing answers that will astonish you.

- *Rule 67:* Know your management—some like a good joke, others only like a joke if they tell it.

- *Rule 68:* Remember that the boss has the right to make decisions. If you think the boss is wrong, tell him or her what you think; but if the boss still wants it done his or her way, do it that way and do your best to make sure the outcome is successful.

Program Planning, Budgeting, and Estimating

- *Rule 73:* Most of yesteryear's projects overran because of poor estimates and not because of mistakes.

- *Rule 74:* All problems are solvable in time, so make sure you have enough schedule contingency—if you don't, the project manager that takes your place will.

- *Rule 79:* Next year is always the year with adequate funding and schedule. Next year arrives on the 50th year of your career.

The Customer

- *Rule 80:* Remember who the customer is and what his or her objectives are (that is, check with the customer when you go to change anything of significance).

Decision Making

- *Rule 82:* Wrong decisions made early can be recovered from. Right decisions made late cannot correct them.

- *Rule 83:* Sometimes the best thing to do is nothing. It is also occasionally the best help you can give. Just listening is all that is needed on many occasions. You may be the boss, but if you constantly have to solve someone's problems, you are working for him.

Professional Ethics and Integrity

- *Rule 85:* Integrity means your subordinates trust you.

- *Rule 86:* Blindsiding the boss will not be to your benefit in the long run.

Project Management and Teamwork

- *Rule 87:* Projects require teamwork to succeed.

- *Rule 88:* Never assume someone knows something or has done something unless you have asked them; even the obvious is overlooked or ignored on occasion, especially in a high-stress activity.

- *Rule 90:* A puzzle is hard to discern from just one piece, so don't be surprised if team members deprived of information reach the wrong conclusion.

Treating and Avoiding Failures

- *Rule 92:* In case of a failure:

  a. Make a timeline of events and include everything that is known.

  b. Put down known facts. Check every theory against them.

  c. Don't beat the data until it confesses (that is, know when to stop trying to force-fit a scenario).

  d. Do not arrive at a conclusion too fast. Make sure any deviation from normal is explained. Remember that the wrong conclusion is a prologue to the next failure.

  e. Know when to stop.

- *Rule 93:* Things that fail are lessons learned for the future. Occasionally things go right: these are also lessons learned. Try to duplicate what works.

- *Rule 94:* Mistakes are all right but failure is not. Failure is just a mistake you can't recover from; therefore, try to create contingency plans and alternate approaches for the items or plans that have high risk.

- *Rule 96:* Experience may be fine but testing is better. Knowing something will work never takes the place of proving that it will.

- *Rule 98:* One of the advantages of NASA in the early days was the fact that everyone knew that the facts we were absolutely sure of could be wrong.

- *Rule 99:* Redundancy in hardware can be a fiction. We are adept at building things to be identical so that if one fails, the other will also fail. Make sure all hardware is treated in a build as if it were one of a kind and needed for mission success.

- *Rule 100:* Never make excuses; instead, present plans of action to be taken.

magic numbers
and percentages

100% of problems left
Mackay 1988

It isn't the people you fire who make your life miserable; it's the people you don't.

100%/85% rule
Common knowledge

Even 100% inspection does not catch all the defects. It is estimated that inspectors using conventional equipment will find only about 85% of all defects.

100%/5%
Simmerman 1993

A study showed that companies could boost profits by about 100% by just retaining 5% more of their customers.

100%
Murphy's Law calendar, 2002

When all 100% fails, read the instructions.

100% = 90% + 90% rule
Zahniser 1993

Ninety percent of the work requires 90% of the time; the remaining 10% of the work requires the other 90% of the time.

90%/10% rule
Common knowledge

Ninety percent of the profit comes from 10% of the customers.

15%–25% rule
Common knowledge

Fifteen percent to 25% of sales income is the price you pay for poor quality.

20%/32% PIMS statistics
Whiteley 1991

The top-level 20% of the business with high customer perception of quality averaged a 32% ROI. The bottom 40% averaged a 14% return on income.

Remark. PIMS is Project Impact of Market Strategy, a project of the Strategic Planning Institute.

90%–96% rule
Furlong 1993

Ninety percent to 96% of unhappy customers won't lodge a complaint.

93.7% "confidence" of Dwayne Phillips
Phillips 1998

If an experienced project manager heads the project, the project is already 93.7% finished.

80/20 principle of software maintenance
Pressman 2001

Twenty percent of all maintenance work is spent "fixing mistakes"; the remaining 80% is spent adapting existing systems to changes in their external environment.

"Out at five" principle of Dilbert
Adams 1996

Work smart for eight hours and go home.

15%/85% concept
Adapted from Deming 1997

1. Eighty-five percent of problems depend on management and only 15% depend on the worker

2. Eighty-five percent of all process problems are due to common cause variation versus 15% that are attributable to special causes

---

19 out of 20
PatentCafe Web site

The sad reality is that 19 out of 20 inventions that are patented by independent inventors are never introduced and sold as a product.

20/20 vision
Phillips 1998

Design is about getting that foresight with the same 20/20 vision as hindsight.

1/4 the cost
Common knowledge

The cost of holding and retaining a current customer is only one-quarter the cost of acquiring a new customer.

"10X" program of IBM
IBM 1990

Ten times improvement (for example, 10 times fewer defects) at every next release.

When does 10 equal 100?
Unknown

When one takes the taxes out of a dollar.

The method 315 approach
Schenck 1994

Method 315 lets you view a situation from different perspectives: user profiles, work flow analysis, organizational profiles, and opportunity appraisal.

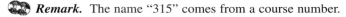 *Remark.* The name "315" comes from a course number.

Zero defects is a reality
Otis and Carey 1992

L.L.Bean filled 500,000 catalog orders for the firm's outdoor gear without an error during the spring of 1992. During 1991, the firm claims that it never fell below 99.9% accuracy in filling customer orders.

1:60 Principle
Mishnah

Something that appears less frequently than 1:60 is of "no consequence." If an item is one-sixtieth or less of a mixture/group, it can be discounted (ignored).

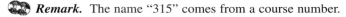 *Remark.* The Mishnah is the section of the Talmud consisting of the collection of oral laws edited by Rabbi Judah ha-Nasi.

50/50 collaboration
Unknown

General practice teaches this: One thinks up the problem, the other solves it.

———•·•———

When does 3 equal 1?
Baker and Baker 1998

People + Resources + Time = Budget

Part Two

Improvement Tools and Techniques

A person who first eats the slightly rotten apples, keeping the good ones for later, has a good chance of eating rotten apples all his life.

—Max Bluvband 1968

People who are only good with hammers see every problem as a nail.

—Maslow 1966

Theory of ones: one activity/one person/ one place/at one time
Adapted from Harrington, Esseling, and Nimwegen 1997

It needs to be questioned why a process cannot be done in one activity, by one person, in one place, or, better still, at one time with no human intervention. This approach leads to the minimum quantity of units you are trying to optimize.

One step before applying preventive measures
Bluvband 1996

When the quality cost is too high (which it usually is!), a small increase in prevention cost will substantially decrease total quality cost. *Prevention* is the operative word.

One step before applying prevention, appraisal activities increase.

Before implementing preventive measures, it is very important to understand what to prevent and how to prevent it. At this stage, the appraisal cost increases. After you have obtained insight as to the sources of the problem, you take preventive measures, thus increasing the prevention cost. Ultimately, the total quality cost is reduced.

First precontrol setup rule
Shainin 1984

When initiating the setup of a machine or a process, as a first step, five pieces should be in a row inside the target precontrol lines (precontrol lines are calculated for target value 50% of the tolerance).

(See also *Five precontrol running rules*, p. 142.)

First principle of judo
Thompson and Jenkins 1993

Don't resist your opponent. Instead, move with him and redirect his energy.

🐾 *Remark.* This is one of the important change management techniques.

The only way to success
SEI 1997

Don't just diet for a week or two; change your lifestyle.

Two causes of variation
Common knowledge

1. *Common cause.* A cause of random deviation that is typical for the existing (regular and usual) distribution function. The failure distribution is not changed.

2. *Assignable cause.* A factor that contributes to variation and is related to a nonrandom or nontypical event that influences the process. The failure distribution is changed significantly.

Two extremes of the spectrum of defect analyses
Lyu 1996

1. Statistical defect models:

   - Abstract

   - Quantitative

   - Distant from the designer

   - Low cost

   - Capable of automation

   - Restricted to a few domains

2. Root cause analysis:

   - Down to earth

   - Qualitative

   - Viewed from the programmer's perspective

   - High cost

   - Human intensive

   - A wide range of domains

Two quality improvement cycles
Adapted from Imai 1986

1. Plan–do–check–act (PDCA)

2. Standardize–do–check–act (SDCA)

Two classifications of organizations' business processes
Harrington, Esseling, and Nimwegen 1997

1. Product business process improvement (PBPI)

2. Administrative business process improvement (ABPI)

Deming's motto in two words
Deming 1997

Reduce variation.

Two types of complexity
Senge 1990

1. Detail complexity

2. Dynamic complexity

Two choices in pursuing personal mastery
Senge 1990

1. Be true to your own vision

2. Be committed to the truth

Effective communication is a two-way street
Bluvband 1998

This is unlike radio transmission, in which one side only broadcasts and the other side only hears.

Three rules for changing huge organizations
Stone 2001

1. Have a simple uplifting message that you repeat over and over

2. Use colorful stories in plain English

3. Praise and reward people who are doing what you want, and don't waste one minute looking for fraud, waste, or abuse

---

Three Cs of successful project organizations
Baker and Baker 1998

1. Communication

2. Cooperation

3. Coordination

Three times to use brainstorming
Common knowledge

1. When a broad range of options is desired

2. When creative, original ideas are required

3. When the participation of the entire group is desired

Three quality cost categories
Common knowledge

1. *Prevention costs.* Those efforts devoted to keeping defects from occurring.

2. *Appraisal costs.* Those efforts devoted to maintaining quality levels by means of formal evaluations, inspections, and tests.

3. *Failure costs.* Those efforts devoted to products that do not meet specifications or that fail to meet the customer's expectations; often broken down into internal and external components.

Three steps that should be taken to reengineer a process
Hammer and Champy 1994

1. Select a process

2. "Understand" the current process:

   • What it does

   • How well (or properly) it performs

   • What the critical issues that govern its performance are

3. Move quickly to redesign

Three dimensions of performance
Bredrup and Bredrup 1995

1. *Effectiveness.* To what extent customer needs are met.

2. *Efficiency.* How economically the resources of the company are utilized.

3. *Changeability.* To what extent the company is prepared for future changes.

Three reasons for doing preventive maintenance
Smith 1993

1. To prevent failure
2. To detect the onset of failure
3. To discover a hidden failure

Three-step model of business decisions
McQuarrie 1993

1. What's going on?
2. What are the options?
3. Which option is best?

Three possible states of a controlled process
Common knowledge

1. Nonstable and not in control
2. Stable and not in control
3. Stable and in control

Three process capability indices
Adapted from Bossert 1996

1. *Cp:* The capability index for a stable process, defined as

$$\frac{USL - LSL}{6\sigma}$$

where USL = Upper Specification Limit and LSL = Lower Specification Limit

Remark. CR (the capability ratio for a stable process) = $\frac{6\sigma}{USL - LSL}$.

2. *Cpk:* The capability index that measures capability at the specification limit that has the highest chance of a part beyond the limit. Defined as the minimum (CPL, CPU).

   CPL: The lower capability index, defined as $\dfrac{\overline{X} - LSL}{3\sigma}$

   CPU: The upper capability index, defined as $\dfrac{USL - \overline{X}}{3\sigma}$

3. *Cpm:* The capability index that takes into account the location of the mean, defined as

$$\frac{USL - LSL}{6\sqrt{\sigma^2 + (\mu - T)^2}}$$

Remark. If instead of Sigma, we'll use the total standard deviation S that takes into account both within-lot and between-lot variation, then instead of capability indices Cp, Cpk, CPL, CPU, and Cpm, we'll get so-called "performances indices" Pp, Ppk, PPL, PPU, and Ppm accordingly.

Three main objectives of lean manufacturing
Liker 1998

1. Zero defects

2. Zero inventory

3. Zero wasted time

Three fundamental selling truths
McCormack 1984

1. Know your product

2. Believe in your product

3. Sell with enthusiasm

Three rules for learning more about people you are dealing with
McCormack 1984

1. Watch and listen

2. Keep your eyes peeled and your ears open

3. Keep your mouth closed

Three main types of evidence to back up your point
Ehrlich and Hawes 1984

1. Statistics

2. Examples

3. Quotations

Three attributes of a good measurement system
Lyu 1996

1. Orthogonality

2. Consistency across phases

3. Uniformity across products

Three Ps of the improvement process
Pande, Neuman, and Cavanagh 2000

1. *Planning:* Determining actions and resources

2. *Piloting:* Trying solutions on a limited scale

3. *Problem prevention:* Ensuring that your team has thought through as many possible difficulties as it can

Four types of benchmarking
Cortada and Woods 1995

1. Competitive

2. Functional

3. Internal

4. Strategic

Four levels of the documentation hierarchy
Common knowledge

1. *Quality manual:* Refers to *what*

2. *Quality procedure:* Refers to *what, who,* and *when*

3. *Work instruction:* Refers to *what, who, when,* and *how*

4. *Record:* Refers to the *forms* and *results*

Four balanced lifecycle cost analysis structures
Adapted from Bluvband 1996, 1997

1. *CBS:* Cost breakdown structure

2. *WBS:* Work breakdown structure

3. *PBS:* Product breakdown structure

4. *QBS:* Quality breakdown structure

Four levels of evaluation of training program (Kirkpatrick model)
Kirkpatrick 1994

1. Reaction

2. Learning

3. Behavior

4. Results

Four rules for person on call to remember to be polite
Martin 1997

1. Don't accept invitations to seated dinners, weddings, or other highly structured events

2. Don't carry a noisemaking beeper anyplace where noise is disruptive

3. Plan ahead so that your exit is unobtrusive

4. Warn your hosts in advance that you may be called away

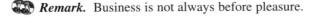 *Remark.* Business is not always before pleasure.

Four Ps of marketing
Mackay 1988

1. Product

2. Price

3. Place

4. Promotion

Four plan–do–check–act (PDCA) cycle activities
Shewhart 1986

1. Plan

    • Assemble a project team

    • Identify the problem or improvement opportunity

    • Plan an experiment to reduce or remove the gap between the desired and actual performance

2. Do

    • Perform the experiment

    • Collect data

3. Check

    • Assess the experiment's results. Study the results. How did the change affect the process?

4. Act

    • If the change did not produce desirable results, return to step 1. If the change improved the process, make it permanent

Remark. The "PDCA cycle" is often referred to as the Deming cycle or the Shewhart cycle.

Four factors that affect productivity
Arthur 1985

1. Changes in each of the inputs

2. Changes in the proportion of each input

3. Differences between full capacity and underutilization of the available capacity

4. Changes in managerial decisions and external factors

Four levels of product complexity
that affect productivity
Brooks 1975

Type of Product	Cost Factor
1. Product	1
2. Programming system	3
3. Programming product	6
4. Programming system product	9

Four kinds of flowcharts as separate tools
Common knowledge

1 Work flowchart diagram

2. Top-down flowchart

3. Arrow diagram

4. Deployment flowchart

Four stages of customer expectations
of a product
Albrecht 1992

1. Basic

2. Expected

3. Desired

4. Unanticipated

Four essential elements of effective management
Hardjono, ten Have, and ten Have 2000

1. *Framing:* Focusing energy and needs. Framing refers to the need to focus energy and efforts (leadership, managing culture, and organizational values).

2. *Alignment:* Coordination by design. Alignment or strategic alignment deals with the issue of coordination by design. It underlines the importance control has for organizations. Without ignoring subjects like change, flexibility, and creativity, the organizations described realize that control is a vital issue in developing effective management practices.

3. *Deployment:* Translating policy into specific objectives. Deployment or policy deployment is aimed at the translation/deployment of long-term policies into concrete, specific objectives and the necessary plans and actions at all organizational levels.

4. *Continuous improvement:* A never-ending process. Improvement and learning are both the cause and effect of sound management (relies heavily on management by fact).

Crosby's four absolutes of quality improvement
Crosby 1996

1. *Conformance to requirements:* The basis of this policy is DIRFT—"Do It Right the First Time." Requirements for quality must be thoroughly understood and accepted.

2. *Prevention:* Quality comes from prevention.

3. *Performance standards:* These must be "zero defects," not "that's close enough."

4. *Measurement:* Measuring by statistics during the company's work process is valuable and should be done.

Juran's four elements of cycle time optimization
Juran 1992

1. *Diagnosis of cycle time:* Analysis of total cycle time and the time consumed by the vital few steps

2. *Diagnosis of the process:* Analysis of how the process has been designed and operated

3. *Diagnosis of major influences:* Analysis of "major influences"— powerful forces that are all-pervasive and must not be ignored, even if it means changing the culture

4. *Identification and implementation of remedies to reduce cycle time:* Improvements in process and technology

---

Juran's four types of quality teams
Adapted from Juran and Gryna 1993

1. *Quality project team* (quality improvement team): Managers, professionals, and workforce from multiple departments (four to eight members); solves cross-functional quality problems

2. *Quality circle* (employee involvement group): Primarily workforce from one department (six to twelve members); solves problems within a department

3. *Self-managing team* (self-supervising team; semiautonomous team): Primarily workforce from one work area (six to eighteen members); plans, executes, and controls work to achieve a defined output

4. *Business process quality team* (business process management team; process team): Primarily managers and professionals from multiple departments (four to six members); plans, controls, and improves the quality of a key cross-functional process

Four major steps in quality cost analysis
Dobbins 1995

1. List all major activities

2. For each activity:

   • List all input: What? From where?

   • Determine value added: Why do it?

   • List all output: What? Where?

3. For each activity:

   • Determine customer requirements

   • Determine supplier requirements

   • Determine measurements

4. For each activity:

   • Analyze measurement requirements

   • Determine level of effort and estimate cost of effort

   • Divide cost into categories

Four stages of group formation and the development cycle
Adapted from Kogan Page 1993

1. *Infancy ("forming"):* Here group members are finding out who others are. There may well be confusion and anxiety as different styles and needs become evident, and potential rivalries may show themselves.

2. *Adolescence ("storming"):* Having set a base level of similarities and expectations, the group will move into a stage where conflicts develop. By working through the issues openly, the group will gain eventual cohesiveness and endurance.

3. *Adulthood ("norming and performing"):* At this stage the group begins to pull together. There is now genuine seeking of

agreement, the development of trust, a give-and-take approach to finding roles, functional relationships, and ways of getting tasks done, despite individual differences (norming). As increasing time and energy are devoted to achieving the team's goals, the ensuing success also has a powerful bonding effect (performing).

4. *Transformation:*

   • Redefinition of the group—the establishment of a new purpose, new goals or a new structure

   • Termination or breakup of the group

Four stages of team development
Adapted from ASQ's Foundations in Quality Learning Series 2001

1. *Forming:* Start-up. The goal is to become familiar with the team's mission, process, and members.

2. *Storming:* The honeymoon is over. The goal is to recognize the need for cohesion and reestablish the team goal.

3. *Norming:* Fine-tuning stage. The goal is to shift the focus to task completion.

4. *Performing:* Competence and cohesion. The goal is to complete the task.

Four issues on which to screen customers for profit potential
Geddes 1993

1. High profit margin

2. Risk of market

3. Competition in market

4. Growth in market

Four scales of the Myers-Briggs Type Indicator (MBTI)
Myers and Myers 1987

1. EI (E = extroversion, I = introversion)

2. SN (S = sensing, N = intuition)

3. TF (T = thinking, F = feeling)

4. JP (J = judging, P = perceiving)

Four types of sampling procedures
Adapted from Bossert 1996

1. For isolated or unique lots or a lot from an isolated sequence

2. For a continuous stream of lots

3. For continuous sampling plans

4. For special plans

Four steps in problem solving
Russel 1990

1. Problem definition

2. Measurement focus

3. Solution

4. Action

Four tips from an industrial engineer on reducing the cost of any job
Meyers 1999

1. Eliminate the unnecessary. Eliminate *muda* (any cost that does not add value to your product).

2. Combine jobs and eliminate movement, storage, delays, and some handling time.

3. Change the sequence of work elements to create a more efficient job, operation, or plant.

4. If you can't do the above three steps, you can always simplify the job by moving items closer and downgrading work elements to produce more work in less time with less effort.

Four standard performance-based metrics
TL 9000, 1999

1. Provide industry performance information for benchmarking

2. Improve telecommunications processes and products

3. Identify customer–supplier improvement opportunities

4. Standardize customer report cards or assessments

Five phases of improving a business process
Harrington, Esseling, and Nimwegen 1997

1. Organizing the improvement

2. Understanding the process

3. Streamlining the process

4. Focusing on implementation, measurements, and controls

5. Focusing on continuous improvement

Five steps of a well-developed technical training program
Fisher 1995

1. Analysis

2. Design

3. Development

4. Implementation

5. Evaluation

Five error-proofing principles
Nakajo and Kume 1985

1. *Elimination:* Eliminate the possibility of error. For example, redesign the process or product so that the task is no longer necessary.

2. *Replacement:* Substitute a more reliable process for the worker. Such as, use robotics (for example, in welding or painting).

3. *Facilitation:* Make the work easier to perform. For example, color code parts.

4. *Detection:* Detect the error before further processing. For example, develop computer software that notifies the worker when the wrong type of keyboard entry is made (for example, alpha versus numeric).

5. *Mitigation:* Minimize the effect of the error. For example, utilize fuses for overloaded circuits.

Five "whys"
Common knowledge

This is a technique for discovering the root cause(s) of problems and showing the relationships of the causes by repeatedly asking the question "why?"

———•·•———

Five-step approach to conflict resolution
Birsner and Balsley 1982

1. Listen or read carefully

2. Defuse the situation and depersonalize the situation

3. Check to see whether a conflict exists

4. Evaluate the importance of the outcome for all the parties involved

5. Select one of the six basic ways to resolve conflict

Remark. For step 5, see *Six basic ways to resolve conflict*, p. 149.

———•·•———

Five steps to help people grow
Blanchard 1986

1. *Tell* (directive): Tell them what to do, how to do it, where to do it, and when to do it.

2. *Show perspective:* Set clear goals. Give them a model of what good results look like.

3. *Let them try* (supportive): Let them try it on their own.

4. *Observe* (supportive): Be there to support, correct, and give feedback as needed.

5. *Praise progress* (supportive): Don't wait for perfection. Praise anything plausible and/or redirect.

Five-point Likert scale format
ASQ's Foundations in Quality Learning Series 2001

Developed by Rensis Likert in 1932, the scale represents a bipolar continuum and gives customers the opportunity to respond in varying degrees. The high end represents a positive response, while the low end represents a negative response. A benefit of this scale is that it offers accurate calibration of respondent answers. Of all customer satisfaction scales, it is the most frequently used.

Examples of Likert-type response formats

I am satisfied with ALD's service.

Strongly disagree	Disagree	Neither agree nor disagree	Agree	Strongly agree
			X	

What do you think about the cashier's service?

Very dissatisfied	Dissatisfied	Neither satisfied nor dissatisfied	Satisfied	Very satisfied
	X			

Five applications of the Pareto chart
Common knowledge

1. When analyzing data by groups to reveal unnoticed patterns

2. When trying to focus on the most significant problem or cause

3. When communicating with others about your data

4. When relating cause and effect by comparing a Pareto chart classified by cause with one classified by effect

5. When evaluating improvement by comparing before-and-after data

Five keys to the effective use of quality costs
Unknown

1. Kind of report

2. Breakdown by cost area

3. Pinpointing of problem areas

4. Measurement of individual elements

5. Effective use of newly gained knowledge

Five criteria of quality customer service
Unknown

1. Reliability

2. Response

3. Knowledge and safety

4. Identification

5. Environmental

Five times to use a checksheet
Unknown

1. When collecting data regarding events, problems, defects, defect location, defect causes, and so forth

2. When collecting data from a production process

3. When data can be observed and collected repeatedly by the same person or at the same location

4. When standardizing a long list of actions, such as multiple preventive maintenance checks on a piece of equipment

5. When data collection can occur at any step of the project

Five important factors in business process analysis
Harrington, Esseling, and Nimwegen 1997

1. Cost

2. Profits

3. Financial risk and importance

4. Products

5. Quantities

———•·•———

Five-M model
Common knowledge

1. Manpower

2. Machine

3. Milieu (environment)

4. Management

5. Mission

———•·•———

Five stages of the benchmarking process
Karlof and Ostblom 1993

1. Decide what to benchmark

2. Identify benchmarking partners

3. Gather information

4. Analyze

5. Implement for effect

Five steps to effective problem solving
Common knowledge

1. Identify the problem

2. Quantify the problem

3. Identify the cause(s)

4. Take action to correct the cause(s)

5. Follow up to ensure that the action taken was effective

Five ways to increase productivity
Unknown

1. Reduce production costs

2. Improvise management methods

3. Understand the work instruction

4. Reduce expenditures

5. Work efficiently

Five characteristics that define a quality circle
Common knowledge

1. A group of about ten members

2. Connected to one organization framework

3. Including a guide and employees

4. Employed in the same profession area

5. Who participate on a volunteer basis

Five applications of quality cost
Constructed

1. A sensitive measurement of the effectiveness of an overall quality effort

2. A positive measurement of a quality assurance manager's effectiveness in integrating these effects

3. A means to effectively establish a program to meet overall needs

4. A means to determine the amount of specific effort that is economically optimum

5. A medium that translates many of the intangibles of quality into a great common denominator

---

Five attribute charts
Common knowledge

1. p chart: Fraction defective

2. np chart: Number of defectives

3. c chart: Number of defects

4. u chart: Number of defects per unit

5. $100p$ chart: Percentage defective

Five precontrol running rules
Shainin 1984

1. If the first piece is within target (50%), run (don't measure the second piece)

2. If the first piece is not within target, check the second piece

3. If the second piece is within target, continue to run

4. If both pieces are out of target, adjust the process and go back to setup

5. Any time a reading is out of specification, stop and adjust

(See also *First precontrol setup rule*, p. 118.)

Five cost estimation methods
Common knowledge

1. Analogy

2. Cost-to-cost

3. Engineering assessment

4. Parametric modeling

5. Subject matter expert

Five reasons for internal failure costs
Common knowledge

1. Scrap

2. Rework

3. Retest

4. Downtime

5. Productivity losses

Five steps for developing a customer satisfaction questionnaire
Hayes 1991

1. Present current standing of customer satisfaction

2. Identify important customers' requirements

3. Monitor satisfaction levels over time

4. Provide organizational comparisons

5. Determine program effectiveness

Five stages of forced change
Unknown

1. Denial

2. Anger

3. Bargaining

4. Depression

5. Acceptance

Five components of robust organizational system engineering (ROSE)
Bluvband 2000

ROSE consists of five components (the rose petals):

1. Organization and process mapping

2. Business-critical parts decomposition and analysis

3. Process failure modes, effects, and causes analysis (PFMECA)

4. Selection of the best possible (optimal) process parameter's values

5. Implementation, testing, analysis, and fixing (ITAAF)

Five guidelines for agenda negotiation
Karrass 1993

1. Don't accept the other person's agenda without thinking about the consequences.

2. Consider where and how issues can best be introduced.

3. Schedule the discussion of issues to give yourself time to think.

4. Study your opponent's proposed agenda for what it deliberately leaves out.

5. Be careful not to imply that your "must" demands are negotiable. You can show your resolve early by not permitting such items into the discussion.

Five steps of the nominal grouping approach
Mears 1995

1. The facilitator presents an issue and explains that ideas will be anonymously submitted.

2. Individual members write down their ideas.

3. Ideas are "shuffled" and recorded on the board.

4. After all ideas are recorded, there is a discussion for the purpose of clarification and evaluation.

5. Individuals anonymously rank order the ideas. The "group decision" is the pooled outcome.

Five types of benchmarking
Mears 1995

1. *Internal:* Benchmarking within the organization or its branches

2. *Competitive:* Comparing key competitive characteristics with those of other companies

3. *Shadow:* Monitoring key product and service attributes of a successful competitor

4. *Industrial:* Comparing within the same industry

5. *World-class:* Comparing processes across diverse industries

Five stages of benchmarking
Spendolini 1992

1. Determine what to benchmark

2. Form a benchmarking team

3. Identify benchmark partners

4. Collect and analyze benchmarking information

5. Take action

Five steps of the *kaizen* movement
Imai 1986

- *Step 1.* Straighten up:
  - Work-in-process
  - Unnecessary tools
  - Unused machinery
  - Defective products
  - Papers and documents
- *Step 2.* Put things in order.
- *Step 3.* Keep the workplace clean.
- *Step 4.* Make it a habit to be clean and tidy.
- *Step 5.* Follow procedures in the workshop.

Five Ws and one H
Imai 1986

1. *Who*
   - Who does it?
   - Who is doing it?
   - Who should be doing it?
   - Who else can do it?
   - Who else should do it?
   - Who is doing the three *mu*s? (See *Three*-mu *checklist of* kaizen *activities*, p. 28.)
2. *What* (Substitute *What* for *Who* with appropriate changes.)
3. *Where* (Substitute *Where* for *Who* with appropriate changes.)
4. *When* (Substitute *When* for *Who* with appropriate changes.)
5. *Why* (Substitute *Why* for *Who* with appropriate changes.)
6. *How* (Substitute *How* for *Who* with appropriate changes.)

Five Ss
Imai 1986

1. Sorting

2. Simplifying

3. Sweeping

4. Standardizing

5. Self-discipline

Five important trends in key processes of management
Hines et al. 2000

1. The decentralization of decision making

2. The need to integrate the business

3. The development of empowerment and a team-based approach

4. The development of an "open organizational system" that interfaces with the environment and is adaptive to prevailing conditions—capable of changing competitive priorities quickly

5. The concept of customer service

Five important areas in process improvement results
Common knowledge

1. Quality

2. Productivity

3. Cycle time

4. Predictability

5. Profitability

Five hints for creating a climate of open communication
Constructed

1. Be open and honest

2. Never be personally critical

3. Share information, ideas, concerns, and problems

4. Listen and respect the integrity of others

5. React as a mature manager to "bad news" as well as to "good news"; that is, don't react too negatively or too personally

---

Five steps of the DEVSA prevention system
Russell 1990

1. Define

2. Evaluate

3. Validate

4. Systematize

5. Act

Five key secrets to mastering successful speech
Ehrlich and Hawes 1984

1. Establish eye contact

2. Speak up

3. Slow down

4. Say words clearly

5. Banish space fillers

Six basic ways to resolve conflict
Birsner and Balsley 1982

1. *Changing perceptions:* Change a negative perception of a situation to a positive one.

2. *Avoiding conflict:* This strategy should be used only when the problem is not critical; otherwise avoidance will aggravate the problem.

3. *Smoothing:* Emphasize areas of agreement and deemphasize areas of disagreement.

4. *Forcing:* Impose your viewpoint upon the other party. This is a win–lose situation as it can cause resentment.

5. *Compromising:* Divide up the common areas of interest and then divide the resources. This strategy may also be a win–lose technique as it contains the risk that one or more of the parties may feel that they were the losers in the compromise.

6. *Confronting and problem solving:* Focus on solving the problem. This strategy calls for a consensus in respect to identifying the problem.

Six ways to make good choices
Adapted from Silber 1998

1. Don't waste much time on trivial decisions

2. Set a deadline for collecting options

3. Narrow down your options

4. Keep an eye on the long-term effects

5. Don't let the fear of a poor choice keep you from making a choice at all

6. Check your response

Six prerequisites for updating documents
Unknown

1. The pages to be added

2. The pages to be removed

3. The date of distribution

4. The date of the previous changes

5. The number of changes to be made

6. The number of previous changes

Six often-used brainstorming evaluation criteria
Unknown

1. Effectiveness

2. Feasibility

3. Capability

4. Cost

5. Time requirement

6. Enthusiasm (of the team and of others)

Six ways to improve quality and to achieve excellence
Unknown

1. Encourage personal commitment to quality by explaining to employees its potential for improving the company's competitive capability

2. Integrate quality operations within the strategic plan

3. Ensure that suppliers and customers are aware of the improvement goals and ensure their involvement

4. Demonstrate what collaboration is to your employees

5. Train your employees to expand and enhance their knowledge

6. Motivate your employees by expending appreciation, not money

---

Juran's six methodology steps for reducing cycle time
Adapted from Juran 1992

1. Define a process

2. List all activities

3. Flowchart the process

4. List the elapsed time for each activity

5. Identify non-value-adding tasks

6. Eliminate all possible non-value-adding tasks (including all rework)

Six classic problem-solving steps
Wortman and Carlson 1999

1. Identify a problem in your work area

2. Define the problem

3. Investigate the problem

4. Analyze the problem

5. Solve the problem

6. Confirm the results

Six basic *hoshin kanri* principles
Bechtell 1995

1. Align the organizational goals

2. Focus on the vital few strategic gaps

3. Work with others to close the gaps

4. Specify the methods and measures to achieve the strategic objectives (note that in this effort, the results are important, but so are the methods used to achieve the results)

5. Make the linkage between local plans transparent

6. Improve the planning process continuously

Six strategies for dealing with resistance to change
Kotter and Schlesinger 1979

1. Educate and communicate the change

2. Enlist employee participation in the project

3. Initiate support efforts, such as training or counseling

4. Negotiate change deployment

5. Use manipulation to obtain support

6. Use threats or direct force

Six steps to Six Sigma
Adapted from Motorola 1996

1. Identify the product you create or the service you provide

2. Identify the customers for your product or service and determine what they consider important

3. Identify your requirements to empower you to provide a product or service that will satisfy the customer

4. Define the work process

5. Mistake-proof the process and eliminate wasted effort

6. Ensure continuous improvement by measuring, analyzing, and controlling the improved process

Six criteria for good project goals
Baker and Baker 1998

1. Specific

2. Realistic

3. Time consistent

4. Measurable

5. Agreed upon

6. Responsibility attributable

Six W questions for management
Common knowledge

1. What?

2. Where?

3. When?

4. Who?

5. Which way?

6. Why?

(See also *Five Ws and one H*, p. 146.)

Six tips for effective listening
Karrass 1993

1. Give your full attention. You just can't listen and do something else at the same time.

2. Don't interrupt.

3. Discourage cute side remarks and distractions.

4. Don't cut off listening when something hard comes up.

5. Practice listening to ideas you don't like. Try to repeat what you've heard.

6. Let the other person have the last word.

Six basic steps to building a house of quality (quality function deployment)
Adapted from Day 1993 and GOAL/QPC 1991

1. *Voice of the customer (VOC):* Needs and wants—the *what*s

2. *Competitive analysis:* How well your company is doing relative to competitors—the *why*s

3. *Voice of the engineer (VOE):* Technical solutions and measures—the *how*s

4. *Correlations:* Relationships between VOC and VOE—the *what*s versus the *how*s

5. *Technical comparison:* Your product performance versus your competition—the *how much*es

6. *Trade-offs:* Potential technical possibilities to be defined, analyzed, and decided—the *how*s versus the *how much*es

---

Six reasons for external failure costs
Arthur 1985

1. Defect investigation

2. Rework

3. Retest

4. Downtime

5. Productivity losses

6. Warranty charges

Seven-step reengineering process
Bogan and English 1994

1. Identify the value-added, strategic process(es) from a customer's perspective

2. Map and measure the existing process(es) to develop improvement opportunities

3. Act on improvement opportunities that are easy to implement and are of immediate benefit (these are the so-called low-hanging fruit)

4. Benchmark for best practices to develop solutions, new approaches, new process designs, and innovative alternatives to the existing system

5. Adapt breakthrough approaches to fit your organization, culture, and capabilities

6. Pilot and test the recommended process redesign

7. Implement the reengineered process(es) and continuously improve

---

Seven tools of customer value analysis
Gale 1994

1. The market-perceived quality profile

2. The market-perceived price profile

3. The customer value map

4. The won/lost analysis

5. A head-to-head area chart of customer value

6. A key events timeline

7. A what/who matrix

Seven stages of the product attribute lifecycle
Gale 1994

1. *Latent:* Customers don't even recognize their desire

2. *Desired:* Customers recognize their desire, but no competitor is meeting it

3. *Unique:* Only one competitor has this attribute

4. *Pacing:* The emphasis on this attribute is increasing

5. *Key:* These are the attributes on which the competition is centered

6. *Fading:* The market is placing less emphasis on this attribute

7. *Basic:* All competitors have this attribute

Seven Malcolm Baldrige National Quality Award categories
Malcolm Baldrige National Quality Award Web site

1. *Leadership.* The leadership category examines senior leaders' personal leadership and involvement in creating and sustaining values, company directions, performance expectations, customer focus, and a leadership system that promotes performance excellence. Also examined is how the values and expectations are integrated into the company's leadership system, including how the company continuously learns and improves, and addresses its societal responsibilities and community involvement.

2. *Strategic planning.* The strategic planning category examines how the company sets strategic directions and how it determines key action plans. Also examined is how the plans are translated into an effective performance management system.

3. *Customer and market focus.* The customer and market focus category examines how the company determines requirements and expectations of customers and markets. Also examined is how the company enhances relationships with customers and determines their satisfaction.

4. *Information and analysis.* The information and analysis category examines the management and effectiveness of the use of data and information to support key company processes and the company's performance management system.

5. *Human resource development and management.* The human resource development and management category examines how the workforce is enabled to develop and utilize its full potential, aligned with the company's objectives. Also examined are the company's efforts to build and maintain an environment conductive to performance excellence, full participation, and personal and organizational growth.

6. *Process management.* The process management category examines the key aspects of process management, including customer-focused design, product and service delivery processes, support processes, and supplier and partnering processes involving all work units. The category examines how key processes are designed, effectively managed, and improved to achieve better performance.

7. *Business results.* The business results category examines the company's performance and improvement in key business areas—customer satisfaction, financial and marketplace performance, human resources, supplier and partner performance, and operational performance. Also examined are performance levels relative to competitors.

Juran's seven process elements for total quality success
Juran 1992

1. Quality council

2. Quality policies

3. Strategic quality goals

4. Deployment of quality goals

5. Resources for control

6. Measurement of performance

7. Quality audits

Seven basic quality control tools

ASQ's Foundations in Quality 1998

The seven basic tools help organizations understand their processes in order to improve them. Managers should understand and apply these tools as needed to develop, implement, and monitor a quality system.

1. *Cause-and-effect diagram:* A tool for analyzing process problems. It is also referred to as the Ishikawa diagram and the fishbone diagram. The diagram illustrates the main causes and subcauses leading to an effect, or symptom.

2. *Checksheet:* A simple data-recording device. The checksheet is custom-designed by the user, which allows him or her to readily interpret the results.

3. *Control chart:* A chart with upper and lower control limits on which are plotted values of some statistical measure for a series of samples or sub-groups. The chart frequently includes a centerline to help detect a trend of plotted values toward either control unit.

4. *Flowchart:* A graphical representation of the steps in a process. Flowcharts are drawn in order to better understand processes.

5. *Histogram:* A graphic summary of the variation and distribution of a set of data. The pictorial nature of the histogram depicts patterns that are difficult to see in a simple table of numbers.

6. *Pareto chart:* A graphical tool for ranking causes from the most significant to the least significant. The chart is based on the Pareto principle, which was first defined by Joseph M. Juran in 1950. The principle, named after 19th-century economist Vilfredo Pareto, suggests (in quality practice) that most effects come from relatively few causes; that is, 80% of the effects come from 20% of the possible causes.

7. *Scatter diagram:* A graphical technique to analyze the relationship between two variables. Two sets of data are plotted on a graph, with the y axis used for the variable to be predicted and the x axis for the variable used to make the prediction. The graph shows possible relationships (although two variables might appear to be related when they are not; those who know most about the variables must make that evaluation).

Seven new management and planning tools
Shigeru 1988

These seven key tools address management issues in the organization. These tools work well during the planning phase and are best suited to leading and facilitating teams. Managers should understand and apply these tools on an ongoing basis.

1. *Affinity diagram:* Organizes ideas into natural groupings in a way that stimulates new creative ideas.

2. *Arrow diagram:* Develops the best possible schedule and appropriate controls to accomplish the schedule. An arrow diagram is similar to the critical path method and the program evaluation review technique.

3. *Matrix diagram:* Shows the relationship among various data including the relative strength.

4. *Prioritization matrix:* Determines the highest-priority options or alternatives relative to accomplishing an objective.

5. *Process decision program chart (PDPC):* Identifies all events that can go wrong and the appropriate countermeasures for these events.

6. *Interrelationship diagram:* Displays the relationships between factors in a complex situation.

7. *Tree diagram:* Shows the complete range of subtasks required to achieve an objective.

John Covey's seven habits of ineffective people
Covey 1989

1. Be reactive: doubt yourself and blame others

2. Work without any clear end in mind

3. Do the urgent things first

4. Think win/lose

5. Seek first to be understood

6. If you can't win, compromise

7. Fear change and put off improvement

Seven habits of effective people
Covey 1989

1. Be proactive

2. Begin with the end in mind

3. Put first things first

4. Think win/win

5. Seek first to understand, then to be understood

6. Synergize

7. Sharpen the saw

Seven basic steps of statistical design of experiments (SDE)
Johnson 1982

1. Select a process

2. Identify the output factors of concern

3. Identify the input factors and levels to be investigated

4. Select a design (from a catalogue, Taguchi, or self-created, for example)

5. Conduct the experiment under the predetermined conditions

6. Collect the data (relative to the identified outputs)

7. Analyze the data and draw conclusions

McKinsey's seven-S framework strategy
Rasiel 1999

1. Shared values

2. Strategy

3. Skills (core competitions)

4. Systems (processes)

5. Structure

6. Staff

7. Style (management, culture)

———•———

New seven-S framework
D'Avenie 1995

1. Superior stakeholder satisfaction

2. Strategic soothsaying

3. Positioning for speed

4. Positioning for surprise

5. Shifting strategic intent

6. Signaling strategic intent

7. Simultaneous and sequential strategic thrusts

———•———

Seven steps of process mapping
Motorola 1996

1. Define critical business issue

2. Draw relationship map

3. Identify disconnects

4. Go to a deeper level

5. Determine relevant process

6. Draw process map

7. Complete process analysis

Seven guiding points in the construction of a long-term benchmarking partnership
Karlof and Ostblom 1993

1. Document all agreements and make sure that they are understood and accepted by both parties

2. Treat all information as confidential

3. Never ask for information or data that you would not be prepared to release yourself

4. Be especially meticulous when you are benchmarking a competitor

5. If you collect supplementary benchmarking information by interviewing your partner's customers and suppliers, you must tell them why you are doing so

6. Respect the condition of a benchmarking partner to remain anonymous

7. Do not take advantage of information received for any other purpose than that of a benchmarking study

---

Seven distinct categories of the SI system
NIST Web site

1. *Length (meter):* A meter is defined as the distance traveled by laser light in 1/299,792,458 parts of a second. The speed of light is fixed at 299,792.458 (approximately 300,000) kilometers per second or 186,282.3976 statute miles per second. There are exactly 2.540 centimeters in 1 inch.

2. *Time (second):* A second is defined as the duration of 9,192,631,770 cycles of the radiation associated with a specific transition of cesium atoms as they pass through a system of magnets and a resonant cavity into a detector.

3. *Mass (kilogram):* A kilogram is defined as the weight of a cylinder of platinum iridium alloy kept by the International Bureau of Weights and Measures at Sèvres (France). A duplicate, in the custody of the NIST, serves as the standard for the United States. This is the only base unit still defined by an artifact.

4. *Electric current (ampere):* An ampere is the magnitude of current that, when flowing in opposite directions through each of two long parallel wires separated by one meter in space, results in a force between the two wires (due to their magnetic fields) of 2×10^{-7} newtons for each meter of length.

5. *Temperature (Kelvin):* The thermodynamic or Kelvin scale of temperature has its zero point at absolute zero and has a fixed point at the triple point of water defined as 273.15° Kelvin (0°C, 32°F). The relationship of the Kelvin, Celsius, and Fahrenheit scales is shown below:

$$°F = 1.8(°C) + 32 \qquad °C = \frac{°F - 32}{1.8} \qquad °K = °C + 273.15$$

6. *Light (candela):* A candela is defined as the luminous intensity of 0.00000167 of a square meter of a radiating body at the temperature of freezing platinum.

7. *Amount of substance (mole):* A mole is the amount of substance of a system that contains as many elementary entities as there are carbon atoms in 0.012 kilograms of carbon 12. The elementary entities must be specified.

Seven micro approaches to buyer segmentation
Kotler 1972

1. Geography

2. Demography

3. Psychographics

4. Buyer behavior

5. Volume

6. Marketing-factor

7. Product space

Seven ways to success
Constructed

1. Beat yesterday.

2. Be persistent. Success is never an accident.

3. Don't be disquieted in time of adversity.

4. Get involved.

5. Make your career fun.

6. Be fully committed; let the music out.

7. Work hard. (It's not difficult as long as you get the results you want.)

Feigenbaum's eight stages of the industrial cycle
Feigenbaum 1983

1. Marketing

2. Engineering

3. Purchasing

4. Manufacturing engineering

5. Manufacturing supervision and shop operations

6. Mechanical inspection and functional test

7. Shipping

8. Installation and service

Eight time-management techniques
Constructed

1. Plan the day's work and set priorities

2. Work to agreed and realistic deadlines

3. Do the best you can with what you have

4. Use delegation and shelving of work where appropriate and review tasks as necessary periodically

5. Keep paperwork and records under control

6. Find the passion in what you are doing

7. Support your team, but encourage them to own their own problems

8. Make finishing things a habit

Eight steps for conducting a cost-effectiveness analysis
Shtub, Bard, and Globerson 1994

1. Define the desired goal

2. Identify the mission requirements

3. Develop alternative systems

4. Establish system evaluation criteria

5. Determine the capabilities of alternative systems

6. Analyze the merits of each

7. Perform sensitivity analysis

8. Document results and make recommendations

Eight steps in Pareto analysis
Constructed

1. Define the problem

2. Identify nonconformities

3. Group nonconformities into categories

4. Determine frequencies of categories

5. Calculate the frequency percentage for each category

6. List the categories in descending order of percentage

7. Plot the frequencies from step 6 as a bar chart

8. Choose "the vital few categories" (20%) that cause 80% of the problem occurrence

Remark. Usually, sorting by frequencies is not enough. The best approach is to use an index similar to the Pareto priority index (PPI) (Hartman 1983)

$$PPI = \frac{\text{Frequency of problem} \times \text{Savings from problem solving} \times \text{Success probability}}{\text{Cost of problem solving} \times \text{Time to problem solving}}$$

(*See also* an important example of PPI-type indicator risk priority number [RPN] in part Six, *One-for-all integrated risk priority number*, page 319.)

Eight key instructions for team-oriented problem solving
Ford Motor Company 1999

1. *Use a team approach.* The team should have a champion. Other roles include those of leader, recorder, and facilitator.

2. *Develop a working definition for the problem.* Compare what should have happened with what actually happened. As in PDCA, consider the following questions: How does the process's actual performance differ from its desired performance? Where does detection or identification of the defect happen? What is the defect's source?

3. *Contain the problem.* Stop it from causing damage while the team is trying to fix it. (This assumes that a previously acceptable process has started producing unacceptable results. A sudden increase in rejects is an example.) Containment is similar to quarantine. Quarantine does not cure a disease, but it keeps it from spreading. Find and segregate nonconforming products to prevent their shipment to customers. Shut down manufacturing equipment that is making bad product. Make sure the containment action is effective.

4. *Identify the problem's root cause.* This is like diagnosing the disease. Tools for doing this include the checksheet, Pareto chart, and cause-and-effect diagram. Design of experiments is a quantitative tool for investigating a problem or trying out an improvement. It requires consultation with an industrial statistician or an engineer who knows statistics.

5. *Select a permanent correction for the root cause, and make sure that it works.* This is like curing a disease.

6. *Carry out the permanent correction.* Monitor the process to make sure it is effective. This is like watching a patient to make sure the cure worked.

7. *Prevent the problem from coming back.* This means holding the gains (as in step 4 of the PDCA cycle).

8. *Recognize the team's accomplishments.* Each company has its own procedures for doing this.

Guidelines for the eight-D
problem-solving process
Ford Motor Company 1999

1. *D1:* Prepare for the 8-D process

2. *D2:* Describe the problem

3. *D3:* Contain the symptoms/implement containment actions

4. *D4:* Define/verify the root cause

5. *D5:* Choose and verify a corrective action

6. *D6:* Implement the permanent corrective action

7. *D7:* Prevent recurrence

8. *D8:* Congratulate the team

Eight strategic planning steps
ASQ's Foundations in Quality 1998

1. Develop a vision and statement of purpose for your company

2. Gather data on the environment in which it operates

3. Assess corporate strengths, weaknesses, opportunities, and threats (SWOT)

4. Make assumptions about factors outside company control

5. Establish appropriate goals

6. Develop steps (strategic and tactical) for implementation

7. Evaluate performance against goals

8. Reevaluate the above steps for perpetual use

Eight types of imperfection
Constructed

1. Blemish

2. Defect

3. Bug

4. Nonconformance

5. Fault

6. Flaw

7. Failure

8. Error

Eight kinds of worker errors
Fisher 1995

1. Forgetfulness

2. Misunderstanding

3. Wrong identification

4. Amateurism

5. Willful errors

6. Inadvertent errors

7. Errors due to slowness

8. Surprise errors

Eight principles of Six Sigma
Harry and Schroeder 1999

1. Recognize

2. Define

3. Measure

4. Analyze

5. Improve

6. Control

7. Standardize

8. Integrate

Ten-step quality-planning road map
Juran and Gryna 1988

1. Identify customers

2. Discover customers' needs

3. Translate

4. Establish units of measure

5. Establish measurement

6. Develop product

7. Optimize product design

8. Develop process

9. Optimize: prove process capability

10. Transfer to operations

Remark. A common technique is to apply measurements to each stage.

Ten targets for process improvement
Constructed

1. Productivity

2. Uniformity

3. Supply

4. Cost

5. Reliability

6. Safety

7. Environment

8. Knowledge

9. Flexibility

10. Simplicity

Ten-point approach to a long-term benchmarking effort
Karch 1992/93

1. Provide leadership

2. Adopt a new philosophy

3. Create an executive steering committee

4. Create a support structure

5. Find one or more pioneers who are willing to attempt a study

6. Educate people

7. Communicate

8. Find and use success stories

9. Make benchmarking a part of the planning process

10. Recognize and reward successful benchmarking efforts

Business process improvement's (BPI's) ten fundamental tools
Harrington, Esseling, and Nimwegen 1997

1. BPI concepts

2. Flowcharting

3. Interviewing techniques

4. BPI measurement methods (for cost, cycle time, efficiency, effectiveness, and adaptability)

5. No-value-added activity elimination methods

6. Simulation modeling

7. Process and paperwork simplification techniques

8. Organizational change management

9. Process walk-through methods

10. Cost and cycle-time analysis (activity-based costing)

Ten steps in the customer satisfaction measurement (CSM) process
Naumann and Hoisington 2001

1. Define the objectives

2. Develop the research design

3. Identify the attributes

4. Design the questionnaire

5. Design the sampling plan

6. Pretest the CSM program

7. Gather data

8. Analyze the data

9. Use the data

10. Improve the CSM program

A set of ten tasks performed by people
Unknown

1. Value-added work

2. Necessary work

3. Rework

4. Unnecessary work

5. Nonwork—authorized

6. Nonwork—unauthorized

7. Speaking about work

8. Speaking about anything except work

9. Hearing about work

10. Hearing about everything, but please, not about work

Ten points of the quality improvement process
Tague 1995

1. What do we want to accomplish?

2. Who cares and what do they care about?

3. What are we doing now and how well are we doing it?

4. What can we do better?

5. What prevents us from doing better?

6. What changes could we make to do better?

7. Do it!

8. How did we do? Try again if necessary.

9. If it worked, how can we do it every time?

10. What did we learn? Let's celebrate!

Ten activities of the supplier certification process
Fisher 1995

1. Define and staff the certification team

2. Identify and select the key suppliers that will be part of the program

3. Rate the current suppliers' quality and delivery performance

4. Determine the products and services that the suppliers will be providing under the program

5. Define a contract that lists the products and specifications of the parts selected for the program

6. Conduct an initial supplier certification kickoff meeting

7. Conduct supplier surveys

8. Evaluate scoring and qualifications of the selected suppliers

9. Present certification awards and contracts to the suppliers

10. Follow up and monitor religiously after the award

Ten rules to observe in conducting a project meeting
Baker and Baker 1998

1. Start on time

2. Develop and distribute an agenda of objectives before the meeting

3. Deal with one agenda item at a time

4. Encourage open communication

5. Take notes

6. Establish a time and place for the next project team review meeting

7. Agree on and reiterate any follow-up activities or action items required

8. End the meeting on time

9. Distribute brief minutes to all attendees within two days of the meeting

10. Make sure the action items and responsibilities are indicated in the minutes

Juran and Gryna's eleven criteria for effective objectives
Juran and Gryna 1988

1. *Measurable:* Objectives stated in numbers can be communicated with precision

2. *Optimal as to overall result:* Objectives that "suboptimize" the performance of various activities can damage overall performance

3. *All-inclusive:* Activities with objectives tend to have high priority but at the expense of remaining activities

4. *Maintainable:* Objectives should be designed in a modular manner so that they can be revised without extensive work

5. *Economical:* The value of meeting objectives should exceed the cost of setting up and administering them

6. *Legitimate:* Objectives should have appropriate official status

7. *Understandable:* Objectives should be stated in clear, simple language that is understandable by those who must meet the objectives

8. *Applicable:* Objectives should fit the conditions of use or should include the flexibility to adapt to the conditions of use

9. *Worthwhile:* Meeting the objectives should benefit the organization and be perceived as beneficial by those doing the work

10. *Attainable:* "Ordinary" people should be able to meet objectives with reasonable effort

11. *Equitable:* Since performance against objectives is frequently used for merit rating, objectives should be similar in difficulty of attainment

Eleven streamlining tools for redesigning processes

Harrington, Esseling, and Nimwegen 1997

1. Bureaucracy elimination

2. Value-added analysis

3. Duplication elimination

4. Simplification methods

5. Cycle-time reduction

6. Error-proofing

7. Process upgrading

8. Simple language

9. Standardization

10. Supplier partnerships

11. Automation and information technology

Eleven environmental stresses on electronic equipment

Constructed

1. High temperature

2. Low temperature

3. Thermal shock

4. Mechanical shock

5. Vibration

6. Humidity

7. Salt atmosphere and spray

8. Electromagnetic radiation

9. Nuclear/cosmic radiation

10. Sand and dust

11. Low pressure (high altitude)

---·•·---

Eleven types of inspection
Constructed

1. *Detailed (100%) inspection:* Sorts good pieces from bad pieces

2. *Acceptance sampling:* Classifies lots as to acceptability

3. *Incoming inspection:* Is performed on material obtained from within or outside the company

4. *Process inspection:* Is done between departments of a single company

5. *Final inspection:* Is done by the producer prior to shipment

6. *Precontrol (narrow-limit control):* Determines whether a change in the process is significant enough to either stop or make adjustments

7. *Control sampling:* Is often used to determine whether the process is changing

8. *Repeatability check:* Measures the ability of the instrument to reproduce its own readings

9. *Accuracy inspection:* Measures the effectiveness of inspectors in finding defects

10. *Product auditing:* Assesses the product and process that produced it; may consider defect seriousness

11. *Discovery (exploratory) sampling:* Provides a specified probability that the sample will contain at least one defect based on an assumed frequency

Twelve tips on taking charge of your time
Adapted from Harris and Harris 1985

1. Plan

2. Have a fuller calendar

3. Count the cost

4. Take charge of your space

5. Be prepared

6. Be precise

7. Do chores in terms of time

8. Enjoy things in terms of time

9. Save time

10. Relax

11. Have something to show for your time

12. Live in the present moment

Twelve golden rules of project management success
Baker and Baker 1998

1. Gain consensus on project outcomes

2. Build the best team you can

3. Develop a comprehensive, viable plan and keep it up-to-date

4. Determine how much staff you really need to get things done

5. Have a realistic schedule

6. Don't try to do more than can be done

7. Remember that people count

8. Gain the formal and ongoing support of management and stakeholders

9. Be willing to change

10. Keep people informed of what you are up to

11. Be willing to try new things

12. Become a leader as well as a manager

Thirteen kinds of documents as sources of knowledge
Harrington, Esseling, and Nimwegen 1997

1. Forms

2. Charts

3. Records

4. Computer lists

5. Information on screens

6. Photographs

7. Graphics

8. Books

9. Audiotapes

10. Meters/measuring machines

11. Cash registers/calculators

12. Instruments

13. Spoken word

Crosby's fourteen-step approach to quality improvement
Crosby 1980

1. Management commitment

2. Quality improvement team

3. Measurement

4. Cost of quality

5. Quality awareness

6. Corrective action

7. Zero defects planning

8. Employee education

9. Zero Defects Day

10. Goal setting

11. Error cause removal

12. Recognition

13. Quality councils

14. Doing it all over again

Fourteen good questions to ask as a flowchart is being developed
Constructed

1. Where does the input come from?

2. How does the material or service get to the process?

3. What are the steps of the process?

4. What is the decision at every step?

5. Who makes the decision at every step?

6. What happens if the decision is yes?

7. What happens if the decision is no?

8. Are there more than two possible decisions at this step?

9. Is there anything else that must be done at this step?

10. Where does the product of this step go?

11. What tests or inspections are done at each step of the process?

12. What tests or inspections are done on the process?

13. What happens if the process fails the test or inspection?

14. Where does the product of the process go?

Fifteen analysis and data collection tools
Constructed

1. Requirements, measures, and indicators tree

2. Performance index

3. Stratification

4. Sampling

5. Survey

6. Checksheet

7. Scatter diagram

8. Regression

9. Box and whiskers plot

10. Histogram

11. Kolmogorov–Smirnov test (KST)

12. Chi-square test

13. Normal probability plot

14. Control charts and process capability

15. Run chart and analysis of time series

Sixteen possible characteristic combinations of the Myers-Briggs Type Indicator (MBTI)
Myers and Myers 1987

The MBTI is an indicator of people's differences in attention, information handling, decision making, and lifestyle. It is based on four scales (see *Four scales of the Myers-Briggs Type Indicator*, p. 134). The combination of the letters gives an indication of a person's character, as in the following examples:

- *FPEN:* Sympathetic, tactful; seeks to understand life rather than control it; likes action and variety; values imagination, inspiration, and possibilities

- *ISTJ:* More interested and comfortable when works quietly, without interruption; realistic and practical; is good at analyzing what is wrong with something; structured and organized

- *ENTJ:* Usually good in reasoning and bright talk; decisive, frank, regularly well informed, systematically expanding his/her knowledge base; often may appear more confident than other people with same experience due to ability to see the "big and overall picture"

Eighteen process control chart families
Constructed

1. $\overline{X}$ *(average) and R (range) charts:* A chart for variables, for example, using measurements

2. $\overline{X}$ *(average) and S (sigma) charts:* A chart for variables using standard deviation instead of range

3. *M (median) and R or M and S charts*

4. *Individual $\overline{X}$ and MR (moving range) charts*

5. *Moving average and moving range charts:* Charts that make unweighted averagings of the latest *n* observations in which the current observation replaces the oldest of the previous *n* observations

6. *Exponentially weighted moving average (EWMA) chart, exponentially smoothed, or geometrically weighted charts:* A chart that averages individual observations or subgroup averages from the current and previous data sets with those taken at earlier times given progressively smaller weighting

7. *Cusum (cumulative sum) chart:* A plotting of the cumulative sums of deviations of individual observations or subgroup averages from a reference value, with trends in the chart identified by a decision mask, of which the most popular form is a (truncated) *V* mask

8. *p (percent or proportion of defectives) chart*

9. *np (number of defective units) chart*

10. *c (count) chart*

11. $u = c/n$ *(count per unit) chart*

12. *Q (quality score) chart:* A chart of quality scores, or weighted counts

13. *D (demerit) chart:* A version of a Q chart in which demerits are used as the weight coefficients

14. *Multiresponse chart:* A control chart for evaluating a process in terms of the responses of two or more characteristics combined as a single statistic for the subgroup

15. *Trend chart:* A control chart for evaluating the process level in terms of deviation of the subgroup average from an expected trend in the process level, in which the trend may be determined empirically or by regression techniques

16. *Acceptance control chart:* A graphical method for the dual purpose of evaluating a process in terms of whether or not it is in a state of statistical control with respect to within-sample or within-subgroup variability, and whether it can be expected to satisfy product or service requirements for the characteristic(s) being measured

17. *Modified control chart or control chart with modified limits:* A special case of an acceptance control chart that relates the location of the control limits to the tolerance requirements by equating the "natural process limits," defined as the 3σ limits for individuals, to the tolerance limits, with the control limits then set at

$$\left(3 - \frac{3}{\sqrt{n}}\right)\sigma \text{ or more conservatively, } \left(3 - \frac{2}{\sqrt{n}}\right)\sigma$$

18. *Adaptive control chart:* A chart that is useful for situations in which process adjustments can be made and in which the need for tight adherence to the standard level is important; uses predictive estimates of process levels based on the assumption that the process will continue along its curve path, and calls for process changes in advance to avoid any predicted deviation

Remark. A new charting technique (the Z-chart) was introduced by Z. Bluvband and P. Grabov (1996) as a chart for loss function; that is, establishing the control limits for the quality related losses. The Z-chart allows for significant reduction of the risk of adjustment errors, combining the Taguchi philosophy and process monitoring approach.

Twenty steps in the product development cycle
Constructed

1. Request for product development

2. Review by product planning

3. Kickoff meeting

4. Tentative management approval

5. Development authorization approval

6. Preliminary design

7. Preliminary design review

8. Full-scale development

9. Critical design review

10. Design freeze

11. Prototype manufacture

12. Prototype testing

13. Review and final recommendations by product planning

14. Management approval

15. Final drawings

16. Final design review

17. Production process requirements study

18. Conditional manufacturing release

19. Reproduction manufacturing release

20. Full manufacturing release

Forty inventive principles
Altshuller 1998

1. Segmentation

2. Extraction

3. Local quality (pencil and eraser in one unit)

4. Asymmetry

5. Combining

6. Universality

7. Nesting

8. Counterweight (boat with hydrofoils)

9. Prior counteraction (reinforced concrete column or floor)

10. Prior action

11. Cushion in advance

12. Equipotentiality

13. Inversion

14. Spheroidality

15. Dynamicity

16. Partial or overdone action (because of difficulty of obtaining 100% of a desired effect, achievement of somewhat more or less to greatly simplify the problem)

17. Moving to a new dimension

18. Mechanical vibration

19. Periodic action

20. Continuity of a useful action

21. Rushing through

22. Conversion of harm into benefit

23. Feedback

24. Mediation

25. Self-service

26. Copying

27. Substitution of inexpensive, short-lived object for expensive, durable one

28. Replacement of a mechanical system

29. Pneumatic or hydraulic construction

30. Flexible membrane or thin film

31. Use of porous materials

32. Change of color

33. Homogeneity

34. Rejection and regeneration of parts

35. Transformation of states

36. Phase transformation

37. Thermal expansion

38. Use of strong oxidizers

39. Inert environment

40. Composite materials

Remark. G. S. Altshuller is the father of TRIZ. The acronym represents the Russian words T*eoria reshenia izobretateliskikh zadatch* (theory of inventive problem solving).

magic numbers and percentages

86%/14% precontrol chart
Adapted from Shainin 1984

During precontrol setup, eighty-six percent of measurement results lie between two boundaries ±1.5σ (half a distance from nominal dimension to tolerance limits), with 7% in each of the outer sections for a total of 14%.

80%/20% Pareto rule
Vilfredo Pareto, ninetenth-century Italian economist

Twenty percent of the problems cause 80% of the damage. These problems should be dealt with from the profit point of view.

80/20 principle (complementary Pareto rule)
Bluvband 1999a

Eighty percent of people don't understand 20% of the terms they use.

Remark. For certain groups of people it is true that 80% of them do not understand even 20% of what they are talking about.

1.33 ratio
Common knowledge

The acceptable Cpk (the actual process capability index) is 1.33.

3–6–12 cycle
ASQ's Foundations in Quality 1998

Training efficiency evaluations occur at 3 months, at 6 months, and at 12 months after training. An efficiency evaluation (reaction, learning, behavior, and results) can also be determined during course development, based on the type of data the organization wants to collect.

The teach–practice 7–21 learning cycle theory
ASQ's Foundations in Quality 1998

The number of repetitions required (from 7 to 21) depends on the task and on the person trying to achieve mastery. Individuals are taught a new skill and allowed to practice it in order to learn it. Researchers have discovered that individuals must practice a new skill from 7 to 21 times before the skill becomes part of their thinking process. Once it is in their thinking process, they can teach it to others.

Walk at 125%; work at 110%
Meyers 1999

"Do as I do and as I say" is an easy sell. Walking at 125% demonstrates what you expect of yourself. Your work and walking pace are habits that will not go unnoticed. Working 10% faster than your competition isn't asking much of yourself and will win any race. Walking pace is the most observable characteristic of a work ethic, so walking fast (125%) is a good way to project your sense of urgency and your attitude toward the work ethic.

40–20–40 rule
Adapted from Pressman 2001

A recommended distribution of effort across the definition and development phases is often referred to as the 40–20–40 rule. Forty percent of all effort is allocated to front-end analysis and design. A similar percentage is applied to back-end testing. You can correctly infer that implementation, or coding in case of software (20% of effort) is deemphasized.

100/0 rule
Herbert, *Jacula Prudentum,* 1651

The buyer needs a hundred eyes, the seller not one.

1%/99% rule
Thomas Edison, cited in Yeomans 1985

Invention is 1% inspiration and 99% perspiration.

Part Three

Probability and Statistics

Chance is a word devoid of sense; nothing can exist without a cause.

—Voltaire, cited in Brussell 1970

Statistics are like a bikini—what shows is real, but what's hidden is vital.

—Unknown

Total area under the
probability density function
Common knowledge

The total area under the probability density function equals one. Thus, one is the probability that a certain event will occur.

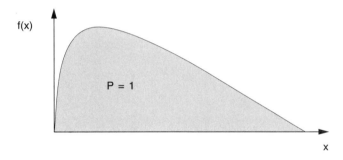

One factor at a time
Common knowledge

For an experiment that is held to assess the influence of a single factor, hold all other factors constant while you vary this one factor. You can thus derive, and learn, the impact of this factor on the whole. Continue evaluating your model. Assess one factor after another by changing the value of the selected factor while all other factors are kept constant.

Remark. A factorial design is much more efficient than a one factor at a time experiment, especially when interactions may be present.

First-order linear model
Common knowledge

$$y = \beta_0 + \beta_1 x_1 + \beta_2 x_2 + \ldots + \beta_k x_k + \varepsilon,$$

where y is the response (the measurable value that is of primary interest; for example, the yield), x_i is the level of factor i, β_i is the regression coefficient to be derived from the test, and ε is the random deviation whose population mean is zero. First-order models cannot account for interaction.

------·•·------

One-way and no-way analysis of variance (ANOVA)
Adapted from Ross 1988

"One-way" ANOVA is one-factor ANOVA: it considers the effect of one controlled parameter upon the performance of a product or process, in contrast to "no-way" ANOVA, in which no parameters are controlled. One-way ANOVA has two components of variation:

- The variation among treatments
- The variation within a treatment (experimental error)
- "No-way" ANOVA also breaks total variation down into two components:
  - The variation of the data average relative to zero
  - The variation of the individual data points around the average (traditionally called experimental error)

⚙ *Remark.* No traditional statistics book mentions no-way ANOVA. Nevertheless, no-way ANOVA takes place in the simplest situation when there is the necessity to analyze a set of experimental data collected.

------·•·------

One method of determining sample size *n*
Adapted from Crow, Davis, and Maxfield 1960

One can derive the sample size n from the minimum total cost expectation (TCE).

TCE = (Risk of accepting H_0 if H_1 is true) × (Cost of accepting H_0 if H_1 is true) + (Risk of accepting H_1 if H_0 is true) × (Cost of accepting H_1 if H_0 is true) + (Cost of experiment) where H_0 is the hypothesis under test and H_1 is the alternative hypothesis.

As n increases, the first two risks decrease and the cost of experiment decreases; thus, the curve of TCE against sample size n may be expected to decrease at first but to increase ultimately.

One-tailed test
Common knowledge

A one-tailed test applies when the alternative hypothesis (H_1) states that the population parameter value—for example, the mean μ—differs from the stated value μ_0 in one direction only:

$$H_1: \mu > \mu_0, \text{ or } H_1: \mu < \mu_0,$$

not $H_1: \mu \neq \mu_0,$

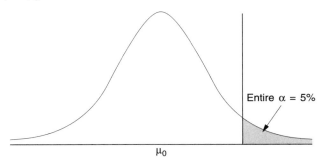

When this is the case, the entire α-risk is placed on one end of the distribution curve.

One-way Kruskal-Wallis ANOVA
Adapted from Winer 1971

The Kruskal-Wallis one-way ANOVA is an analysis of variance by rank. The data (which may even be continuous) are ranked and analyzed without assuming a known (say, normal) population distribution. This type of ANOVA applies to independent samples.

One estimate, two names
Common knowledge

Mean usually stands for the arithmetic mean or arithmetic average. All other "means" consist of two words, such as *geometric mean* and *harmonic mean*. (See also *The three most popular means: arithmetic, geometric, and harmonic*, p. 211.)

Two phases of statistics
Spiegel 1961

The phase of statistics that seeks only to describe and analyze a given group without drawing any conclusions or inferences about a larger group is called *descriptive* or *deductive statistics*.

If a sample is representative of a population, important conclusions about the population can often be inferred from analysis of the sample. The phase of statistics dealing with conditions under which such an inference is valid is called *inductive statistics* or *statistical inference*. Because such an inference cannot be absolutely certain, the language of probability is used in stating conclusions.

Two-way ANOVA
Common knowledge

Two-way ANOVA is an analysis with two factors (A and B). In two-way ANOVA there are three components of variance:

- Factor A treatments
- Factor B treatments
- Experimental error

Two-tailed test
Common knowledge

When a hypothesis is established to test whether a population mean shift has occurred in either direction, a two-tailed test is required:

$$H_1: \mu \neq \mu_0$$

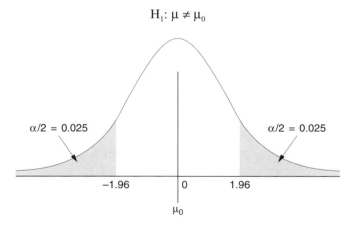

$\alpha/2 = 0.025$ $\alpha/2 = 0.025$

-1.96 0 1.96

μ_0

Second-order model
Common knowledge

$$y = \beta_0 + \beta_1 x_1 + \beta_2 x_2 + \beta_3 x_1 x_2 + \beta_4 x_1^2 + \beta_5 x_2^2 + \varepsilon$$

where y is the response, dependent variable, output, and important result; x_i is the level of the independent variable factor i; ε is random error; and β_i is the regression coefficient estimated from the experiment.

Two widely used applications of the chi-square test

Adapted from Bossert 1996, and Spiegel 1961

1. To test whether the variance of the population under study is equal to the given value σ_0^2 (the hypothetical variance), that is, H_0: $\sigma = \sigma_0$, using the statistics

$$\chi^2 = \frac{(n-1)S^2}{\sigma_0^2}$$

where n is the sample size, S^2 is the obtained variation, and σ_0^2 is the given or hypothetical variance

2. To compare observed and expected frequencies of test outcomes (attribute data) H_0: $O_i = E_i$ (observed frequencies = expected frequencies), using the statistics

$$\chi^2 = \sum_{i=1}^{k} \frac{(O_i - E_i)^2}{E_i}$$

where O_i is the observed frequency for every group, E_i is the expected frequency, and k is the number of considered groups (the possible categories of the sample values)

Two complementary types of statistical hypotheses

Adapted from Crow, Davis, and Maxfield 1960, and Montgomery 1984

We often draw and analyze a sample for the purpose of testing an initial hypothesis, called the *null hypothesis,* or H_0, about the population. A statistical hypothesis is a statement about the parameters of a probability distribution (about the mean, the standard deviation σ, the percentage defective p, and so on). For example, we might state as a null hypothesis that the standard deviation σ is equal to 15 inches, or H_0: $\sigma = \sigma_0$ where $\sigma_0 = 15$ in. The alternative statement H_1: $\sigma \neq \sigma_0$ (or H_1: $\sigma \neq 15$ in.) is called the alternative hypothesis.

As another example, we may think that the mean tension bond strengths of two mortar formulations (modified and unmodified) are equal. This may be stated formally as

$$H_0: \mu_1 = \mu_2, \; H_1: \mu_1 \neq \mu_2$$

where μ_1 is the mean tension bond strength of the modified mortar and μ_2 is the mean tension bond strength of the unmodified mortar. In this case, the statement $H_1: \mu_1 \neq \mu_2$ is the alternative hypothesis to $H_0: \mu_1 = \mu_2$.

To test a hypothesis, we devise a procedure for taking a random sample, computing an appropriate test statistic, and then *rejecting* or *failing to reject* the null hypothesis H_0.

----·----

Two types of errors in hypothesis testing
Common knowledge

1. *Type 1 error:* When the null hypothesis is rejected but is in fact true. The probability of making a type 1 error is called α (alpha) and is commonly referred to as the producer's risk.

2. *Type 2 error:* When the null hypothesis is not rejected but should be rejected. This error is called the consumer's risk and is denoted by the symbol β (beta).

----·----

Two types of error probability
Common knowledge

1. *Type 1 error probability* (α): The probability of an incorrect decision to reject the null hypothesis H_0 (to decide that a shift in process level has occurred) when actually H_0 is true (the process is still in control)

2. *Type 2 error probability* (β): The probability of an incorrect decision to accept null hypothesis H_0 when actually H_1 is true (failing to discover that H_1 is true, deciding that the process is still under control when actually it is not)

Remark. The power of an experiment is defined as the probability P of (rejecting H_0 when it is false) = P of (accepting the aternative to hypothesis H_1 when it is true) = $1 - \beta$, for example, the probability of making the right decision when H_0 is false.

Two complementary terms of measurement quality—1 (general measures/methods)
Common knowledge

1. *Accuracy:* The difference between the average of a number of measurements and the true value; designates the degree of agreement of the measured size with its true magnitude as expressed in standard units of measurement

2. *Precision:* The closeness of the measurement results between themselves when repeated measurements are made of a single unit of product.

Remark. This and the next two pairs of terms are applicable to different fields and have different names, but they have similar meanings.

Two complementary terms of measurement quality—2 (customer opinion/customer survey)
Common knowledge

1. *Validity:* Relates to the question "Is this instrument measuring what we want it (what it is designed) to measure?"

2. *Reliability:* Relates to the question "Would we get the same results if we performed the survey again?"

Two complementary terms of measurement quality—3 (instruments/tools)
Common knowledge

1. *Repeatability:* The ability to repeat the same result by the same operator at or near the same time

2. *Reproducibility:* The closeness of the results of different operators taken at different times

Two terms in relationship analysis between two variables (sets of numbers)
Common knowledge

1. *Correlation:* The degree of linear relationship between two variables

2. *Regression:* A line of relationship between two variables

---

Two kinds of dispersion measures
Spiegel 1961

1. *Absolute dispersion:* This is the actual variation or dispersion as determined from the standard deviation or other measure of dispersion (see *Six measures of dispersion*, p. 222).

2. *Relative dispersion:* If the absolute dispersion is the standard deviation S and the average is the mean $\overline{X}$, the relative dispersion is called the *coefficient of variation* or the *coefficient of dispersion,* as given by Coefficient of variation $= V = \dfrac{S}{\overline{X}}$.

Two main indices of distribution shape
Adapted from Bulmer 1967

1. *Skewness:* Most distributions are unimodal. The main difference in shape among such distributions is in their *degree of symmetry*. Distributions with a right-hand tail longer than the left-hand one are called "skewed to the right," and those with a longer left-hand tail are called "skewed to the left." The most popular numerical measures of this characteristic are Pearson's first and second coefficients of skewness:

$$\text{Skewness}_1 = \frac{\text{Mean} - \text{Mode}}{\text{Standard deviation}} \quad \text{(Pearson's first)}$$

$$\text{Skewness}_2 = \frac{3(\text{Mean} - \text{Median})}{\text{Standard deviation}} \quad \text{(Pearson's second)}$$

2. *Kurtosis:* One can imagine two symmetrical distributions with the same mean and variance, the first of which has long tails and rises to a high, narrow peak and the second of which has short tails and a low, broad peak. The degree of "peakness" of a distribution is usually taken relative to a normal curve, which has kurtosis = 3. One popular kurtosis measure is

$$\text{Kurtosis} = \frac{Q}{P_{90} - P_{10}}$$

where Q is the so-called semi-interquartile range, $Q = (P_{75} - P_{25})/2$, and P_{90}, P_{75}, P_{25}, and P_{10} are the 90th, 75th, 25th, and 10th percentiles for the data.

----·----

Two abbreviations and explanations of design of experiments
Del Vecchio 1997

Choosing the right fraction of many possible experiments to get the most information for the least effort and using whatever method is appropriate to properly analyze the results that come out of those experiments is what is meant by formal design of experiments. The field might be more accurately described as statistically optimized experimentation. The name is very frequently abbreviated to the initials DOE or DOX.

----·----

Two DOE applications
Common knowledge

1. *Off-line:* Design of experiments conducted in an artificial planned environment without the risk of real-time deviations in order to make decisions and then apply them to real production processes

2. *On-line:* A sequential form of experiments conducted in production facilities during regular production using small shifts in factor levels

Two hierarchical terms in DOE
Common knowledge

1. *Factor:* An assignable cause that may affect responses (test results); for example, temperature or color

2. *Level of a factor:* For a quantitative factor such as temperature, a distinct numerical value (for example, 10°F, 20°F, or 30°F); for a qualitative factor such as color, a distinct variation (quality) of the factor (for example, white, black, green, or yellow)

Two types of nested experiments
Common knowledge

1. *Hierarchical:* An experiment to examine the effect of two or more factors in which the same level of a factor cannot be used with all levels of the other factors

2. *Partially nested:* A nested experiment in which several factors may be crossed and other factors nested within the crossed combinations

---

Two major points of the central limit theorem
Common knowledge

If $X_1, X_2, \ldots, X_N$ are independent random variables so that each X_i

1. Has a *finite* mean m_i and variance σ_i^2 and

2. Contributes a *small amount* relative to the sum
$Y_N = X_1 + X_2 + \ldots + X_N$,

then

1. The random variable Y_N tends to *normal distribution,* and

2. The mean M_{YN} and variance V_{YN} of the random variable Y_N may be presented as:

$$\text{mean } M_{YN} = m_1 + m_2 + \ldots + m_N,$$

and

$$\text{variance } V_{YN} = \sigma_1^2 + \sigma_2^2 + \ldots + \sigma_N^2.$$

🌐 ***Remark.*** For a large number N, we can use for Y_N the normal distribution with mean M_{YN} and standard deviation:

$$\sigma_{YN} = \sqrt{V_{YN}} = \sqrt{\left(\sigma_1^2 + \sigma_2^2 + \ldots + \sigma_N^2\right)}$$

Two complementary statistical terms
Common knowledge

1. *Sample mean:* The arithmetic average of the n sample readings

2. *Population mean:* A parameter of the whole population; the
   "center of gravity" of the area under the probability density curve
   for the population

Two cases of estimation of population mean μ
Common knowledge

1. σ known:

$$\text{LCL: } \overline{X} - z_{\alpha/2}\left(\frac{\sigma}{\sqrt{n}}\right)$$

$$\text{UCL: } \overline{X} + z_{\alpha/2}\left(\frac{\sigma}{\sqrt{n}}\right)$$

2. σ unknown:

$$\text{LCL: } \overline{X} - t_{n-1,\alpha/2}\left(\frac{S}{\sqrt{n}}\right)$$

$$\text{UCL: } \overline{X} + t_{n-1,\alpha/2}\left(\frac{S}{\sqrt{n}}\right)$$

where $(1 - \alpha)$ is the confidence level, z is the normal distribution
standardized variable, n is the sample size, t is the Student
distribution, $n - 1$ is the degree of freedom, S is the unbiased
standard deviation estimate from the sample, and (LCL, UCL)
is the confidence interval (lower confidence level, upper
confidence level) for μ.

A pair of terms that describe confidence in an estimation
Common knowledge

1. *Confidence coefficient (confidence level):* The probability that an interval (confidence interval) actually includes the population parameter

2. *Confidence limits (confidence interval):* The endpoints of the interval about the sample statistic that is believed, with a specified confidence coefficient, to include the population parameter

Fits versus bits
Adapted from Kosko 1993

1. *Bit* = Binary unit, 0 or 1 (or yes or no)

2. *Fit* = Fuzzy unit, on a continuum between 0 and 1 (for example, the answer to a question may be 80 percent yes and 20 percent no)

Two types of quality standards
Parsowith 1995

1. *System standards:* Examples are ISO/ANSI/ASQC Q9000 standards and MIL-Q-9858A

2. *Product standards (specifications):* Examples are chemical and physical property requirements and dimensional tolerances

"B" versus "C": comparison of two methods
Bhote 1988

In B versus C analysis, the symbols "B" and "C" stand for two processes or methods or policies that need to be compared. "C" is generally, the current (C) process, and "B" is, supposedly, a better (B) process. But they could also be two new processes. B versus C is a nonparametric comparative experimentation, where no assumption of normality is necessary for either the B or C process.

The power of nonparametric ranking is that it takes only a comparison between extremely small sample sizes from the two processes—often, just three from the B process and three from the C process—to assure, with a very high degree of confidence, that one is better than the other.

Three-D response surface
Common knowledge

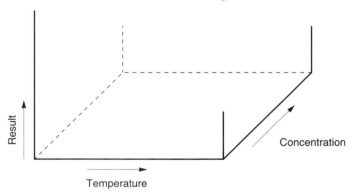

Three types of probability
Common knowledge

1. *Statistical probability:* Based on observed relative frequencies of past occurrences of an event (applies to repeatable events only)

2. *Classical probability:* Derived from a visible symmetry (as with coins and dice)

3. *Subjective probability:* Based on consistent opinions and judgments about an event or on the subject's own degree of belief in the likelihood of an event (applies to any event)

Three tips from Galileo Galilei (measurements)
Adapted from Arthur 1985

1. Count what is countable

2. Measure what is measurable

3. And what is not measurable, make measurable

Three basic entities of measurement methods
Arthur 1985

1. Units

2. Standards of the units

3. Scales that suit the units

Three phases of the customer satisfaction questionnaire
Hayes 1991

1. Determine customer requirements

2. Develop and evaluate the questionnaire

3. Use the questionnaire

Three Ms: measures of central tendency
Common knowledge

1. *Mean:* The arithmetic average of a set of data

2. *Median:* The value that divides a data histogram into two equal areas

3. *Mode:* The value that occurs with the greatest frequency (the most common value)

Relationships between the three Ms
Common knowledge

1. The empirical relation is Mean − Mode = 3(Mean − Median)

2. The relative positions of the mean, median, and mode depend on the frequency curve:

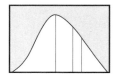 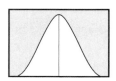 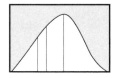

Mode < Median < Mean   Mode = Median = Mean   Mean < Median < Mode

---

Three types of data
Wortman and Carlson 1999

1. *Attribute data:* Data that cannot be measured but can be described in words ("good/bad," "pass/fail") or counted (how many, what percentage, and so on).

2. *Variable data:* Data that can be measured.

3. *Locational data:* Data that answers the question "where?"

(See also *Four levels of measurement scales*, p. 218.)

Third form of data observation
Bhote 1988

The term "nonparametric" is a third form of data observation. In variables data, there is measurement, such a dimension, where there can be a vast number of different readings. In attributes data, there is only "good or bad," "accept or reject." In nonparametric data, there are no measurements as in variables data, but only a ranking of units—from best to worst.

------·•·------

The three most popular means: arithmetic, geometric, and harmonic
Common knowledge

1. *Harmonic mean:* The harmonic mean H of a set of n numbers X_1, $X_2, X_3, \ldots, X_n$ is the reciprocal of the arithmetic mean of the reciprocals of the numbers.

$$H = \frac{n}{\dfrac{1}{X_1} + \dfrac{1}{X_2} + \ldots + \dfrac{1}{X_n}}$$

2. *Geometric mean:* The geometric mean G of a set of n numbers $X_1, X_2, X_3, \ldots, X_n$ is the nth root of the product of the numbers

$$G = \sqrt[n]{X_1 \cdot X_2 \cdot X_3 \cdot \ldots \cdot X_n}$$

3. *Arithmetic mean:* The arithmetic mean $\overline{X}$ is defined as

$$\overline{X} = \frac{X_1 + X_2 + \ldots + X_n}{n}$$

Remark 1. The usual relationship between these three averages is as follows:

$$H \leq G \leq \overline{X}$$

Remark 2. An additional popular mean is the root mean square (RMS)

$$\text{RMS} = \sqrt{\frac{X_1^2 + X_2^2 + \ldots + X_n^2}{n}}$$

which is frequently used in electronics, communications, and other physical applications.

🎨 *Remark 3.* The general expression for the mean value $MV(X_1, X_2, X_3, \ldots, X_n)$ of n numbers $X_1, X_2, X_3, \ldots, X_n$ is

$$MV(X_1, X_2, \ldots, X_n) = F^{-1}\left(\frac{F(X_1) + F(X_2) + \ldots + F(X_n)}{n} \right)$$

where F^{-1} is the inverse function for F (Beckenbach and Bellman 1961).

For example, if $F = X^2$, then $F^{-1} = \sqrt{X}$ (and then MV turns into the root mean square), and if $F = \ln X$, then $F^{-1} = e^X$ (and then MV is the geometric mean).

Three columns in the analysis of variance (ANOVA) table
Common knowledge

1. Source of variation

2. Sum of squares (SS)

3. Degrees of freedom (DF)

Three types of factorial experiments
Adapted from Bossert 1996

1. *Full factorial:* In a full factorial experiment every one of the levels of every factor is tested with all levels of every other factor

2. *Factorial with partial confounding:* A factorial experiment with several replicates in which some main effects or interactions confounded in other replicates are free from confounding

3. *Fractional factorial design (fractional replication):* A factorial experiment in which only an adequately chosen fraction of the treatment combinations required for the complete factorial experiment is selected to be run

Three levels of failure-reporting analysis
Common knowledge

1. *Failure mode:* The type of defect that led to the failure

2. *Failure cause:* The product or process weakness of which the consequence is the failure mode.

3. *Failure mechanism:* The chain of physical, chemical, or mechanical events or processes that led to the failure

Three "magic" squares in design of experiments (DOE)
Common knowledge

1. *Latin square:* A design involving three factors in which the combination of the versions of any one of them with the versions of the other two appears once and only once

2. *Greco-Latin square:* A design involving four factors in which the combination of the versions of any one of them with the versions of the other three appears once and only once

3. *Youden square:* A type of block design derived from certain Latin squares by deleting or adding rows or columns so that one block factor remains made up of complete blocks and the second block factor constitutes balanced incomplete blocks

Three of the most common discrete distributions used in sampling plans
Common knowledge

1. *Hypergeometric:* For defectives (defective items, small population)

2. *Binomial:* For defectives (defective items, large population)

3. *Poisson:* For defects (defects per 100 items)

Three defect categorizations
Common knowledge

1. *Type:* Interface, procedure, or capability

2. *Class:* Missing, wrong, ambiguous, extra, or inconsistent

3. *Severity:* Critical, major, or minor

Three types of correlation
Pande, Neuman, and Cavanagh 2000

1. *Positive:* As *x* increases, *y* increases.

2. *Negative:* As *x* increases, *y* decreases.

3. *Curvilinear:* "What goes up must come down." For some factors, a positive or negative correlation may exist up to a certain point at which it turns into the opposite.

Three popular techniques in statistical sampling
Adapted from Arkin 1984 and Hildebrand and Ott 1991

1. *Estimation sampling.* The objective of estimation sampling is to make inferences about one or more population parameters based on observable sample data. These inferences take several related forms. Conceptually, the simplest inference method is point estimation: the best single guess one can give for the value of the population parameter. Other related inference procedures are interval estimation, in which one uses a point estimate and an allowance for random error to specify a reasonable range for the value of a parameter, and hypothesis testing, in which one isolates a particular possible value for the parameter and asks whether this value is plausible given the data.

2. *Acceptance sampling.* Acceptance sampling involves determining an acceptable quality level and taking a certain number of samples, depending on the lot size. If the rejectable conditions found in the taken samples do not exceed a predetermined number, the lot is considered acceptable.

3. *Discovery or exploratory sampling.* Discovery sampling is a fastidious method of sampling, as it is used to disclose even one nonconformance within a given field size. It discloses a needle-in-a-haystack type of situation, such as a single instance of nonconformance in 2 million entries. The purpose of discovery sampling is disclosure, not acceptance or rejection of items under investigation.

Four types of sampling techniques
(for customer satisfaction)
Common knowledge

1. Random sampling

2. Systematic sampling

3. Stratified sampling

4. Cluster sampling

Four steps to increasing awareness
of estimation bias
Raftery 1994

1. Ensure that all appropriate staff has some familiarity with the notions of personal and reporting bias

2. Introduce procedures to incorporate feedback loops into the filing of estimates and forecasts

3. Introduce procedures to ensure that as many assumptions as possible are made explicit, especially when they are assumptions about risk and uncertainty

4. Foster a culture of estimating and forecasting that:

   • Centers on explicitly dealing with risks and uncertainties across portfolios of projects

   • Accepts that some forecasts will prove to be inadequate

Remark. Forecasts that turn out to be too high (and were thus very safe) should be traced with the same type of negative feedback as forecasts that turn out to be too low.

───────

Four basic rules to adhere to when measuring productivity
Adapted from Arthur 1985

1. A variety of purposes requires a corresponding variety of metrics

2. Productivity should refer to an integrated network of input/output ratios

3. Productivity adjustments depend on their sources, the nature of the changes, and the managerial choices for harnessing the benefits

4. Evaluating the effects of productivity changes requires that the network of input/output ratios be supplemented with cost measures

───────

Four TL 9000 performance metrics
TL 9000, 1999

1. Common metrics (C):

   • Number of problem reports (NPR)

   • Problem report fix response time (FRT)

   • Overdue problem report

   • Fix responsiveness measurements (OFR)

- On-time delivery (OTD)
- System outage measurement (SO)

2. Hardware metrics (H):

- Return rates

3. Software metrics (S):

- Software update quality (SWU)
- Release application aborts (RAA)
- Corrective patch quality (CPQ)
- Feature patch quality (FPQ)

4. Services metrics (V):

- Service quality (SQ)

Four coefficients of a linear relationship
Common knowledge

1. *Coefficient of correlation:* A number between −1 and 1 that indicates the degree of linear relationship between two sets of numbers

2. *Coefficient of determination:* A measure of the part of the variance for one variable that can be explained by its linear relationship with a second variable

3. *Coefficient of multiple correlation:* A number between 0 and 1 that indicates the degree of the combined linear relationship of several predictor variables $X_1, X_2, \ldots, X_p$ to the response variable Y; the simple correlation coefficient between the predicted and observed values of the response variable

4. *Coefficient of partial correlation:* A number between −1 and 1 that indicates the degree of relationship of the response variable Y with a single one of the several predictor variables X_i when the linear effects of one or more of the remaining predictor variables have been held at fixed levels; the simple correlation between the residual values of Y and X_i

Four levels of measurement scales
Common knowledge

1. *Nominal.* Data consists of names or categories only. No ordering scheme is possible.
   Statistics: Mode, number of items, chi-square test
   Example: Color

2. *Ordinal.* Data are arranged in some order but differences between values cannot be determined or are meaningless.
   Statistics: Median, percentages, sign test
   Example: Defect severity

3. *Interval.* Data are arranged in order and differences can be found. However, there is no inherent zero starting point and ratios are meaningless.
   Statistics: Mean, standard deviation, t-test, F-test correlation analysis
   Example: Degrees Fahrenheit (temperature)

4. *Rational.* This level is an extension of the interval level that includes an inherent zero starting point. Both differences and ratios are meaningful.
   Statistics: Geometric mean, percent variation, t-test, F-test, correlation analysis
   Example: Product cost

Four main measurement characteristics
Common knowledge

1. *Sensitivity.* The gage should be sensitive enough to detect differences in measurement as slight as one-tenth of the total tolerance specification. Inadequate discrimination will affect both accuracy and precision.

2. *Reproducibility.* Reproducibility is the "reliability" of the gage system or similar gage systems to reproduce measurements. The reproducibility of a single gage is customarily checked by comparing the results of different operators taken at different times. Gage reproducibility affects both accuracy and precision.

3. *Accuracy.* Accuracy is an unbiased true value and is normally reported as the difference between the average of a number of measurements and a true value. Checking a micrometer with a gage block is an example of an accuracy check.

4. *Precision.* The closeness of the measurement results between themselves when repeated measurements are made of a single unit of product. In gage terminology, *repeatability* is often substituted for precision. Repeatability is the ability of the same operator to repeat the same measurement at or near the same time.

Four measures of central location
Adapted from Crow, Davis, and Maxfield 1960

1. *Mean:* The arithmetic average of all the sample readings

2. *Median:* The halfway point in the readings when they have been arranged in order of magnitude

3. *Mode:* The most frequent value of a random variable

4. *Midrange:* The average of the smallest and the largest readings

Hierarchy of four measurement standards
Common knowledge

1. Primary reference standards

2. Transfer standards

3. Working standards

4. Gages, instruments, and equipment used to measure process and product characteristics

Five traditional types of design of experiments
Common knowledge

1. Trial and error

2. Special lots

3. Pilot runs

4. Error of measurement

5. Simple comparison of two factors

Five major uses of
quality cost measurement
Masser 1957

1. As a measure of overall business quality performance

2. As an analytical tool to indicate where quality dollars are being spent

3. As a method to determine the "when, where, and how of quality improvement"

4. As a budgetary tool for forecasting realistic needs for quality improvement

5. As a means to determine the quality level that would provide "optimum benefit to the business and to the customer"

Five findings of the technical assistance research program (TARP)
Adapted from Naumann and Hoisington 2001

1. Thirty percent of customers with problems complain to the direct provider of the product or service

2. Two percent to 5 percent of customer complaints are voiced to the headquarters level

3. Seventy percent to 90 percent of complaining customers will do business with you again if they are satisfied with the way the complaint is handled

4. Twenty percent to 50 percent will do business with you again if they are dissatisfied with the way the complaint is handled

5. Only 10 percent to 30 percent of customers with problems who do *not* complain or request assistance will do business with you again

---

Five more findings of the technical assistance research program (TARP)
Adapted from Naumann and Hoisington 2001

Why Do Customers Quit?

1. Three percent move away

2. Five percent develop other friendships

3. Nine percent leave

4. Fourteen percent are dissatisfied with the product

5. Sixty-eight percent quit because of an attitude of indifference toward them by the owner, manager, or an employee

Five criteria for vendor choice
Constructed

1. Vendor candidacy

2. Vendor survey

3. Vendor selection

4. Vendor audit

5. Vendor rating

Six measures of dispersion
Constructed

1. *Variance:* The average of all the squares of the distances of every one of the sample readings from their common arithmetic mean

2. *Standard deviation:* The root square value from the variance, or the square root of the average of all the squares of the distances of every one of the sample readings from their common arithmetic mean

3. *Range:* The difference between the smallest and the largest readings in the sample

4. *Mean deviation:* The average of all the absolute values of the distances of every one of the sample readings from their common arithmetic mean

5. *Percentile range:* The range of a set of data; for example, 10–90 percentile range = $P_{90} - P_{10}$, where P_{90} and P_{10} are the 10th and 90th percentiles for the data

6. *Probable error:* The deviation Δ_{pe} from the population mean μ such that 50% of the observations may be expected to lie in the interval $\mu \pm \Delta_{pe}$.

Six data-gathering instruments
Constructed

1. *Surveys.* A properly designed questionnaire is used to gather data from a consistent set of standardized questions. Usually, a sampling of the population is selected for use. Interviewers can be used or the questionnaire can be self-administered.

2. *Focus groups.* A small group of individuals (from 2 to 12) is assembled to explore specific topics and questions, typically for a time range of one to two hours.

3. *Face-to-face interviews.* Individual interviews of 30 to 60 minutes in length may be used. This technique can be very time consuming.

4. *Satisfaction/complaint cards.* The return of a card elicits a response from the company, transforming these cards into feedback forms.

5. *Sources of dissatisfaction.* Dissatisfaction can be expressed through a number of channels, such as complaints, claims, refunds, recalls, returns, repeat services, litigation, replacements, downgrades, warranty work, and mis-shipments.

6. *Competitive shoppers.* Shoppers evaluate the company and its competitors. CEOs may call on their own officers to assess the ease of access to customer service and so on.

Six advantages of process stability and statistical control
Constructed

1. The process has known characteristics; its performance is predictable

2. Cost is predictable

3. Regularity of output is an important by-product of statistical control

4. Productivity is at a maximum, cost at a minimum

5. Costs diminish as quality improves

6. The effects of changes in the system can be measured with appropriate speed and reliability

---

Six buyer study variables (micro approach)
Porter 1985

1. Demographics (age, sex, marital status, education, occupation, and income)

2. Psychographic characteristics (activities, interests, and opinions)

3. Language

4. Purchasing process

5. Purchase occasion

6. Potential buyers

Seven statistical ways to present the same data
Constructed

1. *Arithmetic average:* Presenting a value influenced mainly by the largest values in the data (pulling up)

2. *Geometric average:* Presenting a value influenced mainly by the smallest values in the data (pulling down)

3. *Median:* Presenting a value that divides the data 50–50 (half of the figures are smaller and half are bigger than the median value)

4. *Mode:* Presenting a value that is the most frequently met in the data

5. *Confidence interval–confidence level:* Presenting the estimated endpoints of the interval that is believed, with a specified confidence level, to include the population mean

6. *Tolerance limits:* Presenting the estimated endpoints of the interval that is believed, with a specified probability P, to include the specified percentage of the entire population from which the data was sampled

7. *Graph of the data figures:* Presenting the data as a set of points above and beneath the zero line in accordance with their value and in relation to the value of an indepentend variable as ordinate (for example, time) with defined scale parameter (for example, 100 hours/in.). It is possible to get a different impression manipulating with a scale parameter or non-zero value at a conventional zero line.

Remark. An important particular case of the confidence interval–confidence level approach is the one-sided presentation, such as: "minimum mean time between failures (MTBF) is 1000 hours with confidence level 90 percent," which means that the real MTBF will be greater than 1000 hours with the probability 90 percent.

Eight methods of obtaining information
Constructed

1. Surveys of department heads

2. Surveys throughout the organization

3. Interviews with department heads

4. Interviews throughout the organization

5. Selected interviews

6. Focus groups

7. Department meetings

8. External benchmarking

Eight nonrandomness patterns in statistical process control (SPC)
Western Electric 1956

1. One point beyond zone A.

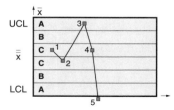

2. Nine points in a row in zone C or beyond

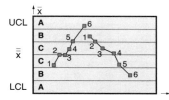

3. Six points in a row steadily increasing or declining

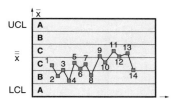

4. Fourteen points in a row alternating up and down

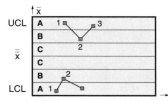

5. Two out of three points in a row in zone A or beyond

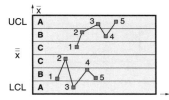

6. Four out of five points in a row in Zone B or beyond

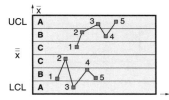

7. Fifteen points in a row in zone C (above and below centerline)

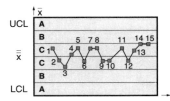

8. Eight points in a row on both sides beyond zone C

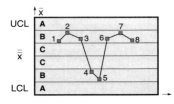

Eight types of frequency curves
Common knowledge

1. *Symmetrical or bell-shaped.* Examples: Normal distribution, student distribution

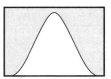

2. *Skewed to the right (positive skewness).* Examples: Weibull distribution, lognormal distribution, gamma distribution

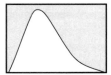

3. *Skewed to the left (negative skewness).* Example: Beta distribution

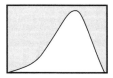

4. *J-shaped.* Example: Truncated part of normal distribution (out-of-tolerance small values removed by inspection)

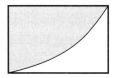

5. *Reverse J-shaped.* Example: Exponential distribution

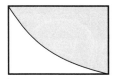

6. *U-shaped.* Example: Beta distribution

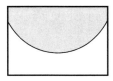

7. *Bimodal.* Example: Mix of two normal populations with significantly shifted population means

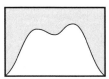

8. *Multimodal.* Examples: Mix of two normal populations with slightly shifted population means, mix of three normal populations

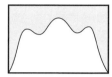

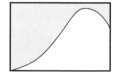 *Remark.* Every one of above frequency curves may be truncated—from one or two sides, for example, truncated normal distribution curve

nine

Nine steps in experimental design
Constructed

1. Problem recognition
2. Problem statement
3. Choice of factors
4. Choice of levels for each factor

5. Selection of the response variable

6. Choice of experiment and experiment planning

7. Performance of the experiment

8. Data analysis

9. Conclusions and recommendations

Ten distributions in statistical quality control
Common knowledge

1. Normal

2. Student (t)

3. Exponential

4. Weibull

5. Chi-square

6. F

7. Poisson

8. Binomial

9. Hypergeometric

10. Pascal, or negative binomial

Ten general dimensions on which to measure quality service
Zeithaml, Parasuraman, and Berry 1990

1. Tangibles

2. Reliability

3. Responsiveness

4. Competence

5. Courtesy

6. Credibility

7. Security

8. Access

9. Communication

10. Understanding of the customer

Eleven questions and statistical answers of 100 top executives about dressing
Molloy 1975

1. *Does your company have a written or an unwritten dress code?* Ninety-seven said yes, 3 said no. Only 2 had a written dress code.

2. *Would a number of men at your firm have a much better chance of getting ahead if they knew how to dress?* Ninety-six said yes, 4 said no.

3. *If there were a course in how to dress for business, would you send your son?* All 100 said yes.

4. *Do you think employee dress affects the general tone of the office?* All 100 said yes.

5. *Do you think employee dress affects efficiency?* Fifty-two said yes, 48 said no.

6. *Would you hold up the promotion of a man who didn't dress properly?* Seventy-two said yes, 28 said no.

7. *Would you tell a young man if his dress was holding him back?* Eighty said no, 20 said yes.

8. *Does your company at present turn down people who show up at job interviews improperly dressed on that basis alone?* Eighty-four said yes, 16 said no.

9. *Would you take a young man who didn't know how to dress as your assistant?* Ninety-two said no, 8 said yes.

10. *Do you think there is a need for a book that would explain to a young man how to dress?* Ninety-four said yes, 6 said no.

11. *Do you think there is a need for a book to tell people in business how to dress?* All 100 said yes.

Fifteen types of information that require data to be stratified

Constructed

1. Products

2. Equipment

3. Workers

4. Materials

5. Shifts

6. Time of day

7. Day of the week

8. Tests

9. Inspections

10. Methods

11. Environment

12. Suppliers

13. Market

14. Measurements

15. Costs

magic numbers and percentages

Percentage under the normal distribution
Common knowledge

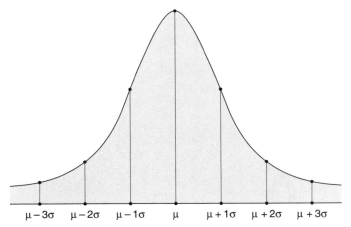

$\mu-3\sigma \quad \mu-2\sigma \quad \mu-1\sigma \quad \mu \quad \mu+1\sigma \quad \mu+2\sigma \quad \mu+3\sigma$

$68.26\% \Leftrightarrow \mu \pm 1\sigma$

$95.45\% \Leftrightarrow \mu \pm 2\sigma$

$99.73\% \Leftrightarrow \mu \pm 3\sigma$

The Six Sigma paradox: the approach guarantees only 97.22% confidence
Constructed

The Six Sigma approach is known to guarantee a fault-free process with the extremely high confidence level of 99.9999998. Formal Six Sigma literature allows for "only" 99.99966 confidence level taking into account

Motorola's assumption that the process mean may drift 1.5σ in either direction. Closer analysis shows that this confidence can be achieved only for the normal probability distribution, while for the unknown or nonnormal distributions, the confidence level may be calculated according to Tchebyshev's inequality:

$$\text{Prob}\left(|X - \mu| \leq k\sigma\right) \geq 1 - \frac{1}{k^2}$$

Thus for Six Sigma, when $k = 6$, the probability $= 1 - \dfrac{1}{6^2} \cong 0.9722$

————

99.7%–0.3% rule

Common knowledge

This rule, well known in SPC assumes 99.7% of production parameters fall within $\pm 3\sigma$ of the centerline, while only 0.3% fall naturally outside the $\pm 3\sigma$ boundaries.

Part Four

Reliability and Risk Assessment

No risk, no fun . . . if there is no risk management.
—Bluvband 1997b

Long after electric starters were standard equipment on American automobiles, hand cranks were still provided.
—Ireson 1966

One for all: dependability
Common knowledge

Dependability is a collective (nonquantitative) term denoting availability performance, as reflected in the following widespread terms: *reliability, maintainability,* and *maintenance (logistics) support performance.*

"One-step-ahead" prediction
Lyu 1996

This is not a long-term prediction. A "one-step-ahead" prediction uses all the data from previous periods of time to predict reliability measures such as mean time to failure and hazard rate for the next period only.

The one most popular distribution in reliability models
Common knowledge

Exponential distribution is the most important reliability distribution. It is used almost exclusively for electronic parts prediction. Why?

- It is simple, as it is completely defined by a single parameter, λ: $R = e^{-\lambda T}$, where T is operating time, R is equipment reliability for the time frame T, and λ is the equipment failure rate

- The failure rate parameter λ is easily estimated

- It is mathematically and physically understandable

- It is additive: if a piece of equipment consists of *n* independent different parts, then the equipment failure rate equals the sum of the failure rates of the parts

- Time-to-failure of the equipment will also be exponentially distributed

- The failure rate is constant and meets the useful life portion of the bathtub curve (see also *Three equipment life periods*, p. 247)

One of the many uses of risk analysis
Raftery 1994

One of the many uses of risk analysis is distinguishing bad luck from bad management and, of course, good luck from good management. In subsequent project postmortems it is possible to distinguish controllable from uncontrollable events.

Two characteristics of risk
Higuera 1995

1. Uncertainty

2. Loss

Risk can travel in two directions
Raftery 1994

The outcome may be better or worse than originally expected. These are known as:

- Upside risks

- Downside risks

Two classes of reliability growth models
Adapted from Kan 1995

1. Time-between-failure models

   - Jelinski-Moranda (J-M) Model

   - Littlewood (LW) Model

   - Goel-Okumoto (G-O) Imperfect Debugging Model

2. Fault-count models

   - Goel-Okumoto Nonhomogeneous Poisson Process (NHPP) Model

   - Musa-Okumoto (M-O) Logarithmic Poisson Execution Time Model

   - Delayed S and Inflection S models (see *Two stages of a testing process*, following)

Two stages of a testing process
Adapted from Yamahada, Ohba, and Osaki 1983

The software defect removal process can be presented as a combination of two stages: defect detection and defect isolation.

Because of the time needed for failure analysis, significant delay can occur between the first failure observation moment and the reporting time. The Delayed S-shaped model and the Inflection S-shaped model for a failure rate curve over time can be regarded as accounting for the programmers and testers learning period with reliability growth, *see next page*.

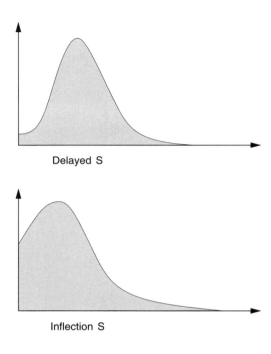

Delayed S

Inflection S

Two types of criticality matrices
Adapted from IEC Std. 62198 2001 and
MIL Std. 1629A 1977

1. European IEC Std. 62198, 2001 Risk Matrix

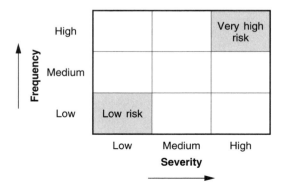

2. Criticality matrix as per MIL Std. 1629A, 1977.

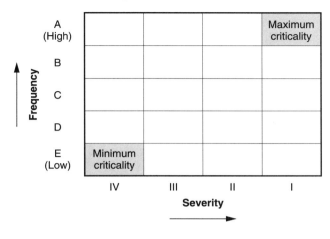

Two types of failure analysis
Common knowledge

1. *FMECA:* Failure mode, effects, and criticality analysis (bottom–up approach)

2. *FTA:* Fault-tree analysis (top–down approach)

Two types of reliability validation
Common knowledge

1. *Reliability demonstration:* An empirical (statistical) test of the hypothesis that the average time-to-failure of equipment operation is acceptable

2. *Reliability qualification:* A preproduction or initial-production hardware test performed to determine design compliance with specified requirements

Two characteristics of survey success
Huck and Cormier 1996

1. Reliability (consistency)

2. Validity (accuracy)

Two complementary safety requirements
MIL Std. 1316E, 1999

1. The system safety failure rate shall be not greater than one per million

2. The system shall not contain any single-point safety failure mode (that is, at least two independent failures, derived from different stimuli, are required to cause a system safety failure)

Remark. The second requirement is needed to prevent the use of "number games" to obtain safety verification: first, prove that the failure rate is low (quantitative analysis), then prove that an occurrence of only one failure is not dangerous (qualitative analysis).

Two R&D phases: the birth and death of a product
Bluvband 1999b

1. Research and development

2. Retirement and disposal

Two basic characteristics of a system: reliability versus safety
Bluvband 1999b

Engineers routinely assume that the more reliable a system is, the safer it is, and vice versa. This assumption is sometimes somewhat erroneous and sometimes very erroneous and leads to a lot of confusion in systems failure analysis. Actually, it is often true that the safer the system, the less reliable it is.

Consider an elevator: The maximum level of safety provides an inoperative elevator—its doors won't shut on you or your dog; pressing buttons won't cause anything unsafe to happen. Enter the inoperative elevator, stay inside as long as you wish, exit it—you are 100% safe. What about reliability? As the inoperative elevator is functionally ineffective, it's absolutely unreliable in getting you up and down to different floors of the building—its reliability is zero.

To improve the safety of a reliable (moving) elevator, designers add elements and controls that limit the probability of its adequate operation. For example, they may add a sensor that indicates proper door closure. If the sensor is out of order, the elevator won't move: reliability decreases while safety improves.

This trivial example demonstrates that in some cases there is an apparent *contradiction* between safety and reliability.

However, in many cases safety and reliability are in full accord. It happens when proper straightforward functioning of a system (just without failures) is enough for both reliable and safe operation. For example, an elevator's mechanical system: the more reliable the mechanics, the more reliable and safer the elevator.

Three components of system effectiveness
Common knowledge

System effectiveness is a measure of the degree to which an item or system can be expected to achieve a set of specific mission requirements successfully. It may be expressed as a function of availability, dependability, and capability:

$$E = A \times D \times C$$

where *A* (availability) is the probability that the system is ready for operation ("up") when called; *D* (reliability, or dependability) is the conditional probability[*] that the system will operate without failure during specified mission time T and mission conditions; and *C* (capability, or design adequacy) is the probability that the system will complete the mission successfully, given no failure at the end of the mission.

[*]*Given the system was "up"—available*

Remark 1. *D* (dependability) can be defined more broadly than just reliability, as the conditional probability that the system will operate without failure (reliability) or be restored on time from failure during specified maximum repair time τ.

Remark 2. System may be available (ready) and reliable (working without any failure), but may complete the mission without success, so be ineffective. For example, an anti-tank missile even being 100% available and 100% reliable, probably will not successfully hit an aircraft, because of inadequate use. In this example $A = 1$, $D = 1$, but $C \approx 0$, then the $E \approx 0$.

Three separate measures of availability
Common knowledge

1. Inherent (potential)

2. Operational (actual)

3. Achieved (final)

Three objectives of risk analysis
Adapted from Ryan 1992

This is not a speculative game at all. Our objective is not to avoid risk but to:

1. Recognize it

2. Price it

3. Sell it

Three risk assessment process steps
Common knowledge

1. Risk analysis

2. Risk evaluation

3. Risk acceptance

Three equipment life periods
Common knowledge

1. *Infant mortality:* The phase related to quality failures—usually a decreasing failure rate

2. *Useful life:* The phase of stress-related failures—an approximately constant failure rate

3. *Wear-out period:* The phase of accumulated damage influence—usually an increasing failure rate

Remark 1. The following terms are also used for the infant mortality period:

- Debugging period (mainly for software products)

- Burn-in period (mainly for systems)

- Screening (mainly for parts and components)

Remark 2. The so called "bathtub curve" (see figure below) shows the hazard rate changes over all three periods forming the system lifetime—from birth to death.

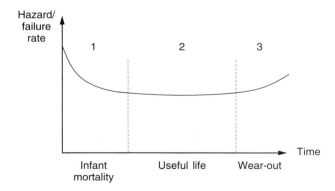

🌐 *Remark 3.* The lower the bathtub curve, the more reliable the useful life period of a system (see figure following, curve B); the longer the bathtub curve, the longer the system's life (see figure following, curve C). From everyday life we know that a person or a thing may have a short but reliable—no illnesses or breakages—useful life period, or on the contrary, one failure may follow another over a very long if unreliable life.

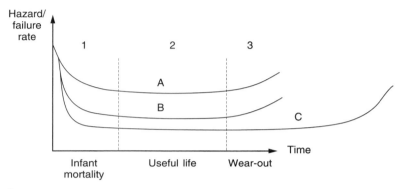

🌐 *Remark 4.* At this point I usually ask my students how the curve continues in time. Their typical answer predicts the failure rate growth with time. Though seemingly logical, this answer is, of course, wrong: at some point of the wear-out period the system failure rate drops to 0—the dead system is ultimately trouble-free (see figure below).

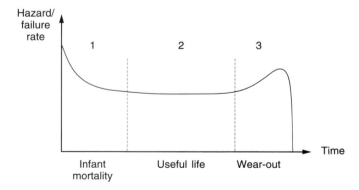

Four risk drivers
Common knowledge

1. Performance risk

2. Cost risk

3. Support risk

4. Schedule risk

Four main categories of risk
Raftery 1994

1. High probability, high impact

2. Low probability, high impact

3. High probability, low impact

4. Low probability, low impact

Four preventive maintenance task categories
Adapted from Smith 1993

1. *Time-directed:* Aimed directly at failure prevention or retardation

2. *Condition-directed:* Aimed at detecting the onset of a failure or failure symptom

3. *Failure-finding:* Aimed at discovering a hidden failure before an operational demand

4. *Run-to-failure:* Aimed on purpose at run to failure because the others are not possible or the economics are less favorable.

Four methods of circuit tolerance analysis
Fuqua 1987

1. *Work case:* All parameters at cumulative worst-case limits

2. *Parameter variation:* Range of variability data

3. *Moment:* Mean values of outputs, variability indices

4. *Monte Carlo:* Statistical simulation

Four actual metrics of maintainability
Adapted from Arthur 1985

1. MTTR (mean time to repair)

2. Downtime per unit time (total downtime per release cycle)

3. Availability per unit

4. Maintenance cost per unit

Five major sources of project risk
Raftery 1994

1. Size

2. Complexity

3. Novelty

4. Intensity (speed of design and construction)

5. Physical location

Five criteria for a model
Kan 1995

1. *Predictive validity:* The capability of the model to predict the number of defects for a specified time period based on the current data in the model

2. *Capability:* The ability of the model to estimate with satisfactory accuracy

3. *Quality of assumptions:* The likelihood that the model assumptions can be met; the logical consistency of the assumptions

4. *Applicability:* The model's degree of applicability across different software products

5. *Simplicity:* The model's degree of simplicity in three aspects:

    • Simple and inexpensive to collect data

    • Simple in concept and does not require extensive mathematical background for software development practitioners to comprehend

    • Readily implemented by computer programs

Five types of maintenance
Constructed

1. *Corrective maintenance:* Repair of failed items

2. *Preventive maintenance:* Protection activity with a purpose to avoid problems before they occur

3. *Perfective maintenance:* Improvement, developing new features

4. *Adaptive maintenance:* Adjustment to new environment, stated features

5. *Productive maintenance:* Production-driven support, extending useful life of production equipment

Remark. Productive maintenance (total productive maintenance) is a lean manufacturing term

Six redundancy techniques
Adapted from Fuqua 1987

1. Simple parallel

2. Duplex

3. Series parallel

4. Parallel series

5. Majority voting

6. Standby

Six dependability management elements
IEC Std. 60300-1, 2001

1. Planning and management

2. Engineering

3. Analysis, evaluation, and assessment

4. Verification and validation

5. Knowledge base

6. Improvement

Six evaluation criteria for occurrences
Constructed

Criteria	Rank	Occurrence
1. Unacceptable	10	Unacceptably high
2. High	9	Extremely High
	8	Very High
	7	High
3. Moderate	6	Moderate-high
	5	Moderate
	4	Moderate-low
4. Low	3	Low
5. Very Low	2	Very Low
6. Remote	1	Remote

Remark. The FMEA team should agree on an evaluation criteria and ranking system, which should remain standardized and consistent for all products and processes of a given type under analysis. For example, for a certain type of product/process, the selected FMEA team may decide that an occurrence value of 1/2 is ranked as unacceptable (10), while the same team dealing with another type of product may rank a much lower occurrence of 1/100 as unacceptably high.

Seven steps of the dependability assurance management function
IEC Std. 60300-1 2001

1. Strategic planning for dependability

2. Allocation of dependability resources

3. Communication of dependability objectives and value

4. Establishment of dependability policy, programs, and associated processes

5. Deployment and control of dependability activities

6. Assessment of dependability performance results

7. Improvement of product/system dependability

Seven sources of risk external to a project
Raftery 1994

1. Inflation

2. Market conditions

3. Cost escalation on input resources

4. Material availability

5. Labor availability

6. Political uncertainty

7. Weather uncertainty

Seven fault-related reliability activities
Constructed

1. Fault tree analysis

2. Fault prevention

3. Fault coverage

4. Fault detection

5. Fault isolation and removal

6. Fault tolerance

7. Fault/failure forecasting

Seven commonly used distributions in RAMS (reliability, availability, maintainability, and safety)
Constructed

Continuous (Time-to-Failure and Time-to-Repair) Distributions

1. Exponential

   • Reliability of electronic components

   • Items without aging

   • Time to replace (maintainability distribution)

2. Normal

   • Reliability analysis of items with wear-out failures (mechanical)

   • Variation of parameters of electronic parts

   • Strength of metallic parts

   • Stress-strength analysis

3. Lognormal

   • Fatigue life of mechanical components

   • Semiconductor failures

   • Time to repair (maintainability distribution)

4. Gamma

   • Time-to-failure distribution of redundant systems

   • Time to second (third, fourth, and so on) failure of a part with exponential distribution

   • Description of either an increasing or a decreasing failure (hazard) rate

5. Weibull

   • Description of either an increasing, a constant, or a decreasing failure (hazard) rate

   • Metal and composite materials strength

Discrete Distributions (Number of Failed or Available Parts)

6. Binomial

   • One-shot device reliability

   • Time-independent part reliability

   • Probability of success

   • Number of failed (defective) parts

7. Poisson

   • Spare parts quantity calculation

   • Distribution of number of failures in a given time interval

   • Number of defects per 100 units

Eight guidelines to increase maintainability/availability
Adapted from Moss 1985

1. *Standardization.* Look for compatibility of matching parts and minimize the number of different parts in the system. This will reduce spare parts inventory.

2. *Modularization.* Have standards for sizes, shapes, and modular units. This will allow for standardized assembly and disassembly procedures.

3. *Functional packaging.* Place all needed components of an item into a kit or package.

4. *Interchangeability.* Control dimensional and functional tolerances. This refers to plug-in devices where spares are instantly interchangeable with failed parts. A part from one unit can be used in other units.

5. *Accessibility.* Allow room for workers to be able to perform the task properly. All items should be accessible. A part should be easy to get to and to replace. Good parts should not be removed to gain access to failed parts.

6. *Malfunction annunciation.* Provide a means to notify the operator when the unit fails. This could include gauges, instrument panels, lights, or sound.

7. *Fault isolation.* A malfunction can be traced. This is the most time-consuming task of all maintenance work. This problem could be minimized by preventive maintenance procedures, built-in test equipment (BITE), simplicity in design of parts, and trained personnel.

8. *Identification.* Have a unique identification for each component and a method of recording corrective and preventive maintenance.

Boehm's eight-task breakdown of risk engineering
Boehm 1996

Risk Engineering:

1. Risk analysis

   • Risk identification

   • Risk estimation

   • Risk evaluation

2. Risk management

   • Risk planning

   • Risk control

   • Risk monitoring

   • Risk directing

   • Risk staffing

Eight capacity elements of ILS (integrated logistics support)
Blanchard 1986

1. Analysis of maintenance support

2. Spare part inventory planning

3. Operation and maintenance manual

4. Manpower and training

5. Foundation planning

6. Packaging, maintenance, and changes

7. Customer support

8. Logistic data bank

Nine steps of risk management
Grey 1995

1. Identify stakeholders

2. Identify key success measures

3. Isolate the baseline project plan

4. Identify issues placing success at risk

5. Assess the issues' likelihood and potential impact

6. Assign ownership

7. Plan risk management

8. Perform aggregate analysis

9. Monitor and review

The nine most frequent sources of risk
Phillips 1998

1. Personnel shortfalls

2. Unrealistic schedules and budgets

3. Development of the wrong software functions

4. Development of the wrong user interface

5. Goldplating (paying too much attention to what the customer wants changed)

6. Continuing stream of changes in requirements

7. Shortfalls in externally furnished components

8. Real-time performance shortfalls

9. Straining of computer science capabilities

Ireson's ten maintenance concerns
Ireson 1966

1. Mission profile

2. Availability and/or reliability requirements

3. Maintenance worker constraints

4. Weight and volume restrictions

5. Spare parts policy

6. Periodic testing

7. Scheduled maintenance

8. Geographic nature of the system

9. Levels of specialized maintenance required

10. Planned types of support equipment

Ten suggested evaluation criteria for severity level ranking

Adapted from QS 9000 1995

10 = Catastrophic without warning
9 = Catastrophic with warning
8 = Very high
7 = High
6 = Moderate
5 = Low
4 = Very low
3 = Minor
2 = Negligible
1 = None

See *Six evaluation criteria for occurrences*, p. 253.

Ten suggested evaluation criteria for detection effectiveness ranking

Adapted from QS 9000 1995

10 = Practically undetectable
9 = Extremely low
8 = Very low
7 = Low
6 = Low-to-moderate
5 = Moderate
4 = Moderately high
3 = High
2 = Very high
1 = Almost certain/certain

Remark. While the meaning of evaluation criteria ranking for detection, occurrence, and severity is different, the ranking logic remains similar, that is, 10—the most undesirable, and 1—the most desirable (see also the remark for the *Six evaluation criteria for occurrences,* p. 253).

Ten elements of lifecycle cost
Constructed

1. Research and development cost

2. Purchasing cost

3. Facilities cost

4. Training cost

5. Manpower cost

6. Test equipment cost

7. Operation and maintenance cost

8. Supply and stock management cost

9. Packaging, handling, storing, shipment, and transportation cost

10. Retirement and disposal cost

Fourteen program performance risk variables
NASA, 1987

1. Technology risks (state-of-the-art advance)

2. Technical risks

3. Material availability risks

4. Testing/modeling risks

5. Integration/interface risks

6. Program personnel risks

7. Software design risks

8. Safety risks

9. Security risks

10. Critical failure mode risks

11. Energy/environmental risks

12. Schedule risks (sensitive to all above-mentioned risks)

13. Cost risks (sensitive to all above-mentioned risks)

14. Supportability risks

Eight Fs and eight Rs of fault tolerance
Constructed

1. *Fault elimination.* Redesigning the product/process so that the task is no longer necessary

2. *Fault prevention.* Minimizing the risk

3. *Fault detection.* Discovering faults prior to use

4. *Fault masking.* Correcting generated errors online

5. *Fault mitigation.* Minimizing the effect of faults

6. *Fault isolation (containment).* Identifying the cause of failure (faulty unit)

7. *Fault zones.* Limiting the faulty unit from causing additional faults

8. *Fault notification.* Informing the operator about the problem

9. *Restart.* Resetting and restarting hardware and software

10. *Reconfiguration.* Switching to an alternative device

11. *Recovery.* Restoring application to condition of operation prior to failure

12. *Repair.* Replacing faulty unit

13. *Reintegration.* Enabling repaired unit without disruption

14. *Replacement.* Substituting a more reliable process (robotics) for a worker (operator)

15. *Resolution and facilitation.* Finding another straightforward solution to exclude any ambiguity during performance

16. *Retry.* Establishing redundancy in time; a chance to make another trial or a couple more trials to achieve success

Eighteen time categories in RAMS

Constructed

T_1	Fault detection time	T_{10}	Administrative time
T_2	Fault location and isolation time	T_{11}	Preventive maintenance time
T_3	Malfunction analysis time	T_{12}	Downtime
T_4	Fault correction time	T_{13}	Free time
T_5	Checkout time	T_{14}	Storage time
T_6	Adjustment time	T_{15}	Non-use time
T_7	Repair time	T_{16}	Readiness time
T_8	Active repair time	T_{17}	Mission (operational) time
T_9	Logistics time	T_{18}	Calendar (total) time

where

$$T_3 = T_1 + T_2$$
$$T_7 = T_4 + T_5 + T_6$$
$$T_8 = T_3 + T_7$$
$$T_{12} = T_8 + T_9 + T_{10} + T_{11}$$
$$T_{15} = T_{13} + T_{14}$$
$$T_{18} = T_{12} + T_{15} + T_{16} + T_{17}$$

These time categories are used to determine reliability, availability, and maintainability.

For example, use availability $A_U = \dfrac{T_{17} + T_{16} + T_{15}}{T_{17} + T_{16} + T_{15} + T_{12}}$

and operational availability $A_0 = \dfrac{T_{17}}{T_{17} + T_{12}}$.

Thirty applicable dependability activities
Adapted from IEC Std. 60300-2 2001

1. Dependability plans

2. Dependability specifications

3. Control of processes

4. Design control

5. Monitoring and review

6. Supply-chain management

7. Product introduction

8. Reliability engineering

9. Maintenance engineering

10. Maintenance support

11. Standardization

12. Human factors

13. Analysis of use environment

14. Reliability modeling and simulation

15. Design analysis and product evaluation

16. Cause–effect impact and risk analysis

17. Prediction

18. Trade-off analysis

19. Lifecycle costing

20. Verification and validation strategy

21. Dependability performance demonstration

22. Reliability growth testing

23. Reliability stress screening

24. Knowledge base establishment

25. Data analysis

26. Data collection and dissemination

27. Dependability records

28. Corrective and preventive actions

29. Upgrade and modification

30. Skills development and enhancement

magic numbers and percentages

63% will fail
Common knowledge

The *mean time to failure* sounds like the midpoint of life, as if the probability of getting to this age were 50/50. In spite of that, only 37% will survive until the mean time to failure; the other 63% of products will fail before that.

99.9% = 0
Common knowledge

If every part is 99.9% good in a unit with 1,000 parts, the probability that the unit is good is actually zero.

The "zero-risk" preference, or the Allais paradox
Raftery 1994

In a large number of empirical studies, it has been shown that very careful people who are well aware of the probability calculus, are rational, and have limited personal capital compared with the sums involved tend to prefer A over B:

- Situation A: Receive a certain $1 million

- Situation B: Receive a lottery ticket with:

  - A 10% chance of winning $5 million

  - An 89% chance of winning $1 million

  - A 1% chance of winning nothing

Remark. The mathematical expectation of the sum to be won in situation B is $1.39 million ($390,000 more than in situation A).

Part Five

Software

In the computer world, hardware is anything you can hit with a hammer; software is what you can only curse at.

—Unknown

Software is like entropy. It is difficult to grasp, weighs nothing, and obeys the Second Law of Thermodynamics; i.e., it always increases.

—Augustine 1987

One is enough within a software procedure
Pressman 2001

A cohesive module should (ideally) do just one thing.

From "one-to-one" to "many-to-one" relationships
Common knowledge

- *One-to-one.* One occurrence of object A can relate to one and only one occurrence of object B, and an occurrence of B can relate to only one occurrence of A. Example: Citizen, social security number

- *One-to-many.* One occurrence of object A can relate to one or many occurrences of object B. Example: Street, noncorner building

- *Many-to-one.* Many occurrences of A can relate to only one occurrence of B. Example: Child, (biological) mother

---

One structure for most estimation models
Common knowledge

The typical structure of an effort E and development time D estimation model is obtained using regression analysis on data collected from past software projects. The usual overall formula is

$$E = a_1 + a_2 \times x^b$$

where x is the primitive (directly measurable or countable parameter) used as an estimation variable. For example, the constructive cost model

(CoCoMo) uses the primitive KLOC (kilos, or thousands, of lines of code). As an illustration of the above-mentioned structure, the CoCoMo for embedded software effort E, applied in person-months, is calculated as follows:

$$E = 3.6 \times (\text{KLOC})^{1.2},$$

that is, $a_1 = 0$, $a_2 = 3.6$, $b = 1.2$, and

$$D = 2.5 \times (E)^{0.32},$$

that is, $a_1 = 0$, $a_2 = 2.5$, $b = 0.32$, where D is the development time in chronological months.

Level one of capability maturity model (CMM) classification
SEI 1994

At level one, capability is a characteristic of the individuals, not of the organization.

Two qualitative criteria of good software design
Pressman 2001

1. Cohesion-relative functional strength of a module

2. Coupling-relative interdependence among modules

Two kinds of bugs
Common knowledge

1. *Error:* An unwanted condition or occurrence that arises during a software process and deviates from its specified requirement

2. *Defect:* An unwanted condition or occurrence that has defied all attempts (inspections, reviews, walk-throughs, tests, and corrective action measures) at elimination during development and so is delivered to the customer

Two views of software quality
Blum 1992

1. *External quality.* External quality sums up the user's feelings about the product. Questions pertinent to external quality are: Does it do everything desired? Does it do it well? Does it make sense? Does it increase the user's ability to do his or her job? This includes factors such as efficiency, human engineering, usability, integrity, correctness, and reliability.

2. *Internal quality.* Internal quality is the developer's view of the software. It looks at software in the long term, directing us to build software that has the lowest possible cost over time. This includes factors such as portability, testability, understandability, modifiability, flexibility, and interoperability.

Two software test strategies
Common knowledge

1. *Top-down:* Using STUBS, a computer program statement, to substitute for the body of a software module that is or will be defined elsewhere

2. *Bottom-up:* Using Drivers, a computer program that controls a peripheral device and, sometimes, reformats data for transfer to and from the device

Two strategies for software testing
Common knowledge

1. *Black box:* Functional testing, which ignores the internal mechanism of a system or component and focuses solely on inputs, outputs, and conditions to evaluate its compliance with specified functional requirements

2. *White box:* Structural testing, which takes into account the internal mechanism of a system or component; includes branch testing, path testing, statement testing, and so on

Remark. Actually these two kinds of testing strategy are two kinds of test case preparation: once test cases are prepared, the testing procedure should be carried out in the same manner, regardless of how the test cases were prepared.

Two assumptions related to the software development process
Kan 1995

1. The defect rate observed during development is positively correlated with the defect rate in the field: the higher the defect rate is during development, the higher will be the field defect rate

2. The more defects are discovered and removed early, the fewer will remain in later stages (given the same error injection rate and defect removal effectiveness)

Two aspects of the software engineering partition
From IEEE Std. 1002-1987. Copyright ©1987 IEEE. All rights reserved.

1. Job function

   • Product engineering function

   • Requirements analysts

- Design
- Coding
- Integration
- Conversion
- Debugging
- Product support
- Software maintenance
- Verification and validation
- Reviews and audits
- Product analysis
- Testing
- Technical management functions
- Process management
- Product management
- Resource management

2. Lifecycle

- Concept phase
- Requirements phase
- Design phase
- Implementation phase
- Test phase
- Qualification phase
- Manufacturing phase
- Installation and checkout phase
- Operations and maintenance phase
- Retirement phase

Two characteristics of data element relationships
Common knowledge

1. *Cardinality:* Cardinality is the specification of the number of occurrences of one object that can be related to the number of occurrences of another object.

2. *Modality:* The modality of the relationship is zero if there is no explicit need for the relationship to occur or the relationship is optional. The modality is one if the occurrence of the relationship is mandatory.

Two types of software configuration audit
Common knowledge

1. *Physical configuration audit (PCA):* The primary intent of the PCA is to verify and ensure that the software and its documentation are internally consistent and ready for delivery (to be sure that all items are available in appropriate configuration and properly integrated). PCA is accomplished after the software acceptance test is run successfully.

2. *Functional configuration audit (FCA):* The primary intent of the FCA is to verify and ensure that the software product actual functionality and performance are consistent with the requirement specifications (evaluating of earlier verification and validation efforts, tracing the requirements from their initial specification, evaluating the consistency between baselined product elements). FCA is accomplished after the software qualification test is run successfully.

Remark. Hardware PCA is verifying that the product, its components, and their integration are in accordance with the appropriate approved drawings and documentation.

Two types of equipment and software application tests
Common knowledge

1. α-test (conducted at the developer's place)

2. β-test (conducted at the customer's site)

Three computer-related products
Common knowledge

1. Hardware

   • Physical material directly involved in performing a specific function (IEC 902 1987)

   • Physical equipment used to process, store, or transmit computer programs or data (IEEE Std. 610.12-1990)

2. Software

   • Intellectual creation comprising the programs, procedures, data, rules, and any associated documentation pertaining to the operation of a data-processing system (IEC 61508-4 1998; ISO 2382-1, 1993)

   • Computer programs, procedures, rules, and any associated documentation and data pertaining to the operation of the computer system (UK MoD Def. Std. 00-55 1997; IEEE Std. 610.12-1990; IEEE Std. 1062-1993)

3. Firmware

- The combination of a hardware device and computer instructions and data that reside as read-only software on that device (UK MoD Def. Std. 00-55, 1997)

Remark. An additional term, *screenware,* can be introduced as a combination of virtual reality, draft proposals, and plans projected on a screen to present an idea that is being sold.

Three basic elements of a good software project plan
Phillips 1998

1. Task list

2. Resources

3. Task network

Three baselines crossed by design
Phillips 1998

1. *Requirements baseline:* This baseline points to everything in the other two design baselines

2. *Allocated baseline:* This baseline contains the high-level design

3. *Design baseline:* This baseline contains the low-level or detailed design

---

Three types of software maintenance
Common knowledge

1. *Corrective maintenance:* Repair of bugs, stated features

2. *Adaptive maintenance:* Adjustment to new environment, stated features

3. *Perfective maintenance:* Improvement, new features

Three elements of OOM paradigm
Adapted from Hetzel 1993

OOM (object-oriented measurement) is the bottom-up (B-U) paradigm based on:

    a. Input measures: resources (people, tools, and so on)

    b. Output measures: deliverables (created products)

    c. Result measures: effectiveness of the deliverables

Remark. The bottom-up paradigm is complementary to the top-down (T-D) paradigm, goals–questions–metrics (GQM), that starts with an identified set of desires and needs (development of *goals*), followed by relevant questions (generation of *questions* that define the goals), and concludes with identification of measures (*metrics*) that answer the questions. In practice, the so-called "sandwich approach" is recommended: move in both directions—T-D and B-U—and integrate the outcomes.

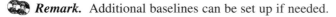

Three levels of baseline in configuration identification
Common knowledge

1. *Functional baseline:* Defines the general requirements of an entire product

2. *Allocated baseline:* Defines the general requirements of a major item in the overall product

3. *Product baseline:* Defines the detailed requirements of an item

Remark. Additional baselines can be set up if needed.

Three safety-critical software categories
From IEEE Std. 1228-1994. Copyright ©1994 IEEE. All rights reserved.

1. Software whose inadvertent response to stimuli, failure to respond when required, response out-of-sequence, or response in combination with other responses can result in an accident

2. Software that is intended to mitigate the result of an accident

3. Software that is intended to recover from the result of an accident

Three software test levels
Common knowledge

1. Unit/component testing

2. Integration testing

3. System testing

Three types of software imperfection
From IEEE Std. 982.2-1988. Copyright ©1988 IEEE.
All rights reserved.

1. *Error:* A problem in the software. Error within the product exists when a desired feature or characteristic is wrong, incomplete, or missing from the software. The source of errors may be either developers or users. Those developer errors resulting in undetected fault in the product directly affect reliability. User errors, usually misunderstandings, can affect perceived reliability.

2. *Fault:* A realization of error that leads to failure or is stopped by some prevention mechanism (redundancy).

3. *Failure:* A realization of fault in the final software output. A failure may occur when a fault is encountered (for example, in the code or the user documentation) or when a how-to-use error is made by the user and there is no redundancy or additional check to avoid the failure in the output result.

See also *Fourth type of product imperfection,* p. 250.

Three abilities of software project planning (per the CMM)
SEI 1994

1. Developing estimates for the work to be performed

2. Establishing the necessary commitments

3. Planning the work

Three CMM-family standards
SEI Web site

1. *CMM:* The Capability Maturity Model, developed by the Software Engineering Institute (SEI), is a well-structured compilation of best practices that can be gradually implemented in software development

2. *CMMI:* Capability Maturity Model Integration merges the software and system engineering

3. *P-CMM:* The People Capability Maturity Model, or People CMM, is a framework that helps organizations successfully address their critical people issues

Three steps to hiding design secrets effectively
McConnell 1996

1. Identify the design secrets to hide. The most common secrets are items that have a high probability of changing.

2. Separate each design secret by putting it in its own unit (package, module, subroutine, or class).

3. Isolate or hide each secret so that if it does change, the change will not affect the rest of the software.

Three Ps of harmony in software development
Phillips 1998

1. *People:* People in this context are all those who influence the project

2. *Process:* The process consists of the steps taken to write the software

3. *Product:* The product is the project's final outcome

Three ranks/degrees of requirement necessity
From IEEE Std. 830-1993. Copyright ©1993 IEEE.
All rights reserved.

1. *Essential:* Implies that the software will not be acceptable unless these requirements are provided in an agreed manner

2. *Conditional:* Implies that these are requirements that would enhance the software product but would not make it unacceptable if they are absent

3. *Optional:* Implies a class of functions that may or may not be worthwhile; gives the supplier the opportunity to propose something that exceeds the software requirement specification

Three questions about each bug you find
Van Vleck 1989

1. Is the cause of the bug reproduced in another part of the program?

2. What "next bug" might be introduced by the fix we're about to make?

3. What could we have done to prevent this bug in the first place?

Three categories of debugging approaches
Myers 1979

1. Brute force

2. Backtracking

3. Cause elimination

Three functional categories of measures
Constructed

1. Product measures:

    a. Errors, faults, and failures

    b. Mean time to failure, failure rate, and reliability growth

    c. Complexity and difficulty (McCabe cyclomatic complexity, function points, and constructive cost model CoCoMo)

2. Process measures:

    a. Management and control

    b. Risk evaluation and cost–benefit analysis

    c. Test coverage and inspection effectiveness

3. Project measures:

    a. Scheduling measures (slip and lead)

    b. Budgeting measures (monthly cumulative budget target and actual cumulative expenditures)

    c. Benefit–cost measures (payback period and internal rate of return)

Three features that characterize orthogonal defect classification
Common knowledge

1. *Independent.* Each of the value classifications needs to be as independent of the others as possible. Since the classifications are semantic they may be "fuzzy," but should be clear.

2. *Distribution changes.* A collection of defects should demonstrate a changing pattern in their distribution as a function of process. The value sets should be collectively exhaustive so that they can explain the position of the product.

3. *Process invariance.* The first two properties should be invariant across most of the software development processes and practices.

Three software quality factors
McCall, Richards, and Walters 1977

1. Operational characteristics

2. Ability to undergo changes

3. Adaptability to new environments

Three categories of software quality cost
Pressman 2001

1. Prevention costs:

   - Quality planning

   - Formal technical reviews

   - Test equipment

   - Training

2. Appraisal costs:

   - In-process and interprocess inspection

   - Equipment calibration and maintenance

   - Testing

3. Failure costs:

   - Internal failure costs

   - Rework

   - Repair

   - Failure mode analysis

   - External failure costs

   - Complaint resolution

   - Product return and replacement

   - Help-line support

   - Warranty work

Four basic elements of configuration management
Adapted from Cox, Blackstone, and Spencer 1995

1. *Configuration identification:* The process of defining and identifying every element of the product

2. *Configuration control:* The management of the change order process from design to implementation

3. *Configuration accounting:* The documenting of the approved configuration identification, status of changes, and implementation status of the changes ("bookkeeping" of the proposed and implemented changes)

4. *Configuration audits:* A review of the product against the engineering specifications to determine compliance

Remark. There are two types of configuration audits: PCA—physical configuration audit and FCA—functional configuration audit (see *Two types of software configuration audit*, p. 276).

IEEE's set of four common design views
From IEEE Std. 1016.1-1993. Copyright ©1993 IEEE.
All rights reserved.

1. Decomposition

2. Dependency

3. Interface

4. Detailed design

Four basics that work in software development
Phillips 1998

1. Balance people, process, and product

2. Promote visibility

3. Organize by using configuration management tools properly

4. Use standards judiciously

Four black box software testing techniques
Common knowledge

1. Equivalence partitioning

2. Boundary-value analysis

3. Cause–effect graphing

4. Error guessing

(See also *Five white box software testing techniques*, p. 293.)

Four types of software tests
Common knowledge

(What feature we are testing)

1. Functional

2. Performance

3. Usability

4. Stress

Four steps for reliability-centered software test (RCST) planning
Bluvband 2002

1. Divide all projects into equivalent families

2. For each family study and match:

   • Appropriate failure intensity function

   • Appropriate "effort scale" (time, manpower)

   • Test/field failure intensity ratio

3. Define the acceptable failure intensity level

4. Plan the effort and translate it to required human resources and expected time-to-release

―――――

Four tips to publishers on how to avoid software bugs
Kaner and Pels 1998

1. Plan realistically

2. Don't drive the programming staff to overwork and get tired

3. Invest in good tools for the staff

4. Reward the staff for reliability, not for speed

―――――

Four phases of software maintainability
Arthur 1985

1. *Planning:* Specifies maintainability requirements and translates them into design criteria

2. *Design:* Establishes the functional and physical characteristics providing maintainability

3. *Measurement:* Verifies quantitative and qualitative maintainability goals

4. *Performance review:* Evaluates the results, providing feedback about the success of the maintainability program

Four software safety requirement analyses
Adapted from IEEE Std. 1228-1994.
Copyright ©1994 IEEE. All rights reserved.

1. *Criticality analysis (system hazard analysis):* Assesses the potential for unacceptable risk of each software requirement specification

2. *Specification analysis:* Evaluates each of the safety-critical software requirements (See *Eighteen safety-critical software requirements*, p. 315)

3. *Timing and sizing analysis:* Evaluates the safety implications of safety-critical requirements that relate to execution time, clock time, and memory allocation

4. *Different software system analyses:* May be required if more than one software system is being integrated

———•+•———

Four types of software maintenance
Wortman et al. 2000

1. *Corrective maintenance:* Acts to correct errors that are uncovered after the software is used.

2. *Adaptive maintenance:* Is applied when changes in the external environment precipitate changes to the software.

3. *Perfective maintenance:* Incorporates changes that are requested by the customer/user community; enhances performance or maintainability.

4. *Preventive (proactive) maintenance:* Improves future maintainability and reliability and provides a basis for future enhancements. Reengineering as a tool for preventive maintenance not only recovers design information from existing software but uses this information to alter or reconstitute the existing system in an effort to improve overall quality.

Four IEEE standard definitions of software maintenance

From IEEE Std. 1219-1992. Copyright ©1992 IEEE.

1. *Adaptive maintenance:* Modification of a software product performed after delivery to keep a computer program usable in a changed or changing environment

2. *Corrective maintenance:* Reactive modification of a software product performed after delivery to correct discovered faults

3. *Emergency maintenance:* Unscheduled corrective maintenance performed to keep a system operational

4. *Perfective maintenance:* Modification of a software product after delivery to improve performance or maintainability

Four types of standards in software engineering

From IEEE Std. 1002-1987. Copyright ©1987 IEEE.

1. Process standards:

   - Method

   - Technique

   - Measurement

2. Product standards:

   - Requirements

   - Design

   - Component

   - Description

   - Plan

   - Report

3. Professional standards:

- Occupational title

- Code of ethics

- Certification

- Licensing

- Curriculum

4. Notation standards:

- Nomenclature

- Representation

- Language

Four recommended software concerns to review
ISO 9000-3, 1997

1. Customer-related concerns

2. Technical concerns

3. Management concerns

4. Legal, security, and confidentiality concerns

Four reasons to use reliability models
Kan 1995

1. Objective statement of the quality of the product

2. Resource planning for the software maintenance phase

3. Tracking of current status

4. Determination of when to end system testing

Four process building blocks (per the CMM)
SEI 1997

1. Software estimation

2. Design

3. Coding

4. Peer review

Four guidelines related to accuracy from the point of view of safety
Hecht and Hecht 2001a

Accuracy and precision are important to safety under the following conditions:

1. Thresholds are approached

2. The algorithms result in taking a small difference between two large numbers

3. The algorithms can result in the possibility of a denominator being sufficiently close to zero to cause an overflow condition in the safety system

4. Iterative algorithms can cause cumulative effects from initially small errors

Four aspects of orthogonal defect classification
Common knowledge

1. Type (How fixed?)

2. Trigger (Catalyst)

3. Impact (So what?)

4. Source (What code?)

Four Cs of software project management
Johnson 1995

Complexity causes confusion and costs.

Fourth type of software imperfection
Bluvband 2002

"Assist request" is the fourth type of software imperfection in addition to error, fault, and failure (see p. 280). It is the state of a software product when assistance is needed for the product's further functioning.

A software failure may be one of the causes of an assist request but not the only one.

Sometimes an expert's assistance is required to make a decision on how to proceed, for example, how to respond to some obscure situation, like the following pop-up query on the screen:

"Loading script C\win98\system\scanreg.vbs" _ "OK?"

The operator is faced with the dilemma of hitting OK or not, fearing that hitting OK could cause a disaster. Obviously, while the operator agonizes whether to hit OK or not, a downtime situation exists. The operator needs assistance to resolve this dilemma and thus terminate the downtime.

Therefore, software reliability and availability are affected by MTBA (mean time between assists), not just MTBF (mean time between failures).

It goes without saying that MTBA ≤ MTBF.

Five content area elements of software requirement specification
Adapted from Phillips 1998

1. *Functionality:* What the software will do

2. *Performance:* How fast and reliably the software will perform its function

3. *Design constraints:* How the software complies with standards and hardware limitations, user interface, operating system, type of computer, programming language, and so on

4. *Attributes:* What the "-ilities" (reliability, maintainability, and so on) of the software are

5. *External interfaces:* How the software will interact with the external hardware and software world

---

Five white box software testing techniques
Common knowledge

1. Statement coverage

2. Decision (path, branch) coverage

3. Loop testing

4. Condition coverage

5. Decision and condition coverage

(See also *Four black box software testing techniques*, p. 286.)

Five areas of effort for analysis of software requirements
Unknown

1. Problem recognition

2. Evaluation and synthesis

3. Modeling

4. Specification

5. Review

Five hints on specifying software quality
Arthur 1985

1. Rely on the vendor

2. Inspect the system when it is delivered

3. Inspect the system at the vendor's premises

4. Actively keep the vendor under surveillance

5. Certify the vendor's quality assurance program

Five examples of software documentation
Constructed

1. Training documentation

2. Online documentation

3. The user's manual

4. The operator's manual

5. The maintenance manual

Five steps and outputs of software quality metrics methodology

From IEEE Std. 1061-1992. Copyright ©1992 IEEE.
All rights reserved.

1. *Establish software quality requirements.* A list of quality factors is selected, prioritized, and quantified at the outset of a system development or system change. These requirements shall be used to guide and control the development of the system and, on delivery of the system, to assess whether the system meets the quality requirements specified in the contract.

2. *Identify software quality metrics.* The software quality metrics framework is applied in the selection of relevant metrics:

   - Approved quality metrics framework

   - Metrics set

   - Cost–benefit analysis

3. *Implement the software quality metrics.* Tools are either procured or developed, data are collected, and metrics are applied at each phase of the software lifecycle.

   - Description of data items

   - Metrics/data items

   - Traceability matrix

   - Training plan and schedule

4. *Analyze the software quality metrics results.* The metrics results are analyzed and reported to help control the development and assess the final product.

   - Organization and development process changes

5. *Validate the software quality metrics.* Predictive metrics results are compared with the direct metrics results to determine whether the predictive metrics accurately measure their associated factors.

Five important areas of software requirement specification (SRS)

From IEEE Std. 830-1993. Copyright ©1993 IEEE.
All rights reserved.

1. *Functionality:* What is the software supposed to do?

2. *External interfaces:* How does the software interact with people, the system's hardware, other hardware, and other software?

3. *Performance:* What is the speed, availability, response time, recovery time, and so on of various software functions?

4. *Attributes:* What are the portability, correctness, maintainability, security, and other considerations?

5. *Design constraints imposed on an implementation:* Are there any required standards in effect, implementation language, policies for database integrity, resource limits, operating environments, and so on?)

(See also *Five content area elements of software requirement specification*, p. 293, and *Eight characteristics of a good software requirement specification (SRS)*, p. 303.)

Five Ws and two Hs of a good software project plan

Boehm 1989

• *Objectives:* Why is the system being developed?

• *Milestones and schedules:* What will be done When?

• *Responsibilities:* Who is responsible for a function? Where are they organizationally located?

• *Approach:* How will the job be done technically and managerially?

• *Resources:* How much of each resource is needed?

Five goals of software development teams
Phillips 1998

1. Clear and simple design

2. Clean and readable code

3. Complete and readable documentation

4. Use of standards

5. Complete easy-to-use test suite (Keep good copies of the tests, test data, and instructions on how to conduct and interpret all the tests. The maintainers will use these time and time again.)

Five rules (three dos and two don'ts) of software project planning
Adapted from Phillips 1998, Humphrey 1995, and Thomsett 1995

• Do use metrics

• Do create plans that succeed

• Do allow some preliminary design

• Don't accept arbitrary plans unless you can negotiate the product

• Don't play estimating games

Five maturity levels of CMM/Trillium standards
Adapted from SEI 1994 and Coallier et al. 1994

1. *Initial/unstructured:* The development process is ad hoc. (Risk: high)

2. *Repeatable/project oriented:* Individual project success is achieved through strong project management planning and control. (Risk: medium)

3. *Defined/process oriented:* Processes are defined and utilized at the organizational level, although project customization is still permitted. (Risk: low)

4. *Managed/integrated:* Process instrumentation and analysis is used as a key mechanism for process improvement. (Risk: lower)

5. *Optimizing/fully integrated:* Formal methodologies are extensively used. Organizational repositories for development history and process are utilized and effective. (Risk: lowest)

Six existing types of software maintenance
Constructed

1. *Adaptive maintenance:* Introduction of modifications to the software to accommodate changes in the external environment

2. *Corrective maintenance:* Reactive modification of a software product, performed after delivery, to correct discovered faults

3. *Emergency maintenance:* Unscheduled corrective maintenance, performed to keep a system operational

4. *Perfective (enhancement) maintenance:* Maintenance that enhances software by adding functions that will provide new benefits for the customer, thus extending the software beyond its original functional requirements

5. *Preventive (predictive) maintenance:* Maintenance that incorporates accumulative knowledge relating to the manner of detecting the onset of failure

6. *Reengineering:* Reengineering of old software either manually or by using a specialized set of CASE (computer aided software engineering) tools to better understand its internal functions and thus improve performance

Six milestones for six baselines
Adapted from Phillips 1998

Baseline	Corresponding Major Milestone
1. *Functional.* What the system must do	PSR (product specification review)
2. *Allocated.* High-level design of system	PDR (preliminary design review)
3. *Design.* Low-level design of system	CDR (critical design review)
4. *Development.* System that satisfies the developers	TRR (test readiness review)
5. *Product.* Off-line system that satisfies the users	QAR (qualification acceptance review)
6. *Operational.* System in use	OAR (operational acceptance review)

Six types of software test attributes
Lyu 1996

1. Test coverage

2. Test sequencing

3. Test interaction

4. Test variation

5. Simple path coverage

6. Combination path coverage

Six system test triggers
Common knowledge

1. Recovery

2. Start and restart

3. Workload volume stress

4. Hardware configuration

5. Software configuration

6. Normal mode

Seven types of software safety code analysis
From IEEE Std. 1228-1994. Copyright ©1994 IEEE.

1. Logic

2. Data

3. Interface

4. Constraint

5. Programming style

6. Noncritical code

7. Timing and sizing

Seven important internal quality factors
Blum 1992

1. Portability

2. Reliability

3. Efficiency

4. Human engineering

5. Testability

6. Understandability

7. Modifiability

Seven indicators of estimation capability
Park 1996b

1. Management acknowledges its responsibility for developing and sustaining an estimation capability

2. The estimating function is supported by a budget and funds

3. Estimators are equipped with the tools and training needed for reliable estimating

4. The people assigned as estimators are experienced and capable

5. Recognition and career paths exist such that qualified people want to serve as estimators

6. Estimators work with process improvement teams to quantify and track progress in software process improvement

7. The estimating capability of the organization is quantified, tracked, and evaluated

Seven types of software errors
Unknown

1. Calculation errors

2. Deviations from specifications

3. Interface-integration errors

4. Hardware interfacing errors

5. User interface errors

6. Error-handling errors

7. Load condition errors

Eight types of software safety design analysis
Adapted from IEEE Std. 1228-1994.

1. *Logic analysis:* Evaluates algorithms and control logic

2. *Data analysis:* Evaluates intended use of each data item

3. *Interface analysis:* Verifies the proper design of interfaces, both internal and external

4. *Constraint analysis:* Evaluates the safety of restrictions imposed on the selected design by the requirements and by real-world considerations

5. *Functional analysis:* Ensures that each safety-critical software requirement is covered and that an appropriate criticality level is assigned to each software element

6. *Software element analysis:* Examines software elements that are not designated safety-critical and ensures that these elements do not cause a hazard

7. *Timing and sizing analysis:* Establishes timing and sizing estimates to allow evaluation of the operating environment; conducted for software safety requirements analysis

8. *Reliability predictions and analysis:* Establishes reliability goals; set by acceptable risk levels

Eight characteristics of a good software requirement specification (SRS)

From IEEE Std. 830-1993. Copyright ©1993 IEEE.
All rights reserved.

1. Correct

2. Unambiguous

3. Complete

4. Consistent

5. Ranked for importance and/or stability

6. Verifiable

7. Modifiable

8. Traceable

Eight defect-type attributes

IBM 1990

1. Function

2. Assignment

3. Interface

4. Checking

5. Timing/serialization

6. Build/package/merge

7. Documentation

8. Algorithm

Eight software quality factors

Adapted from Galin and Bluvband 1995 and
Vincent, Waters, and Sinclair 1988

SFQ #	Software Quality Factor	Definition	Metric
1	Correctness	• The extent to which a program satisfies its specifications and fulfills the user's mission objectives	• Faults/lines of code • Faults relative to requirements and standards
2	Efficiency	• The amount of computing resources and code required by a program to support a function	• Actual utilization/ allocated utilization
3	Flexibility	• The effort required to modify an operational program	• Average labor days to change
4	Integrity	• The extent to which access to software or data by unauthorized persons can be controlled	• Faults/lines of code • Faults relative to security
5	Interoperability	• The effort required to couple one system with another	• Effort to couple/ effort to develop
6	Maintainability	• The effort required to locate and fix a defect in an operational program	• Average labor days to fix
7	Portability	• The effort required to transfer a program from one hardware configuration and/or software system environment to another	• Effort to transport/ effort to develop
8	Reliability	• The extent to which a program can be expected to perform its intended function with the required precision	• Faults/lines of code

Eight tips about symptoms
Adapted from Pressman 2001 except as noted

1. The symptom and the cause may be geographically remote

2. The symptom may disappear (temporarily) when another error is corrected

3. The symptom may actually be caused by nonerrors (for example, round-off inaccuracies)

4. The symptom may be caused by human error that is not easily traced

5. The symptom may be a result of timing problems rather than processing problems

6. It may be difficult to accurately reproduce input conditions (for example, a real-time application in which input ordering is indeterminate)

7. The symptom may be intermittent (especially in embedded systems that couple hardware and software inextricably)

8. The symptom may be due to causes that are distributed across a number of tasks running on different processors (Cheung, Black, and Manning 1990)

Eight review inspection triggers
Common knowledge

1. Backward compatibility

2. Lateral compatibility

3. Design conformance

4. Concurrency

5. Logic flow

6. Side effects

7. Documentation

8. Rare situation

Nine criteria for a mature software process
SEI 1994

1. Defined

2. Documented

3. Trained

4. Practiced

5. Supported and maintained

6. Controlled

7. Verified and validated

8. Measured

9. Able to improve

Nine checklists for review of software requirements

Hecht and Hecht 2001b

Table 1 Checklist for standard review plan.

Software Requirement Specification (SRS) Topic	Example
Site adaptation requirements	Consistency with design basis
Product function (overview)	Traceability to system requirements
Regulatory requirements	Correctness and verifiability of SRS statements
Redundant operation	Completeness with respect to design basis
Audit functions	Verification of access
Criticality of the application	Prioritization of requirements in the SRS
Safety and hazards analysis	Completeness with respect to design basis
Physical security requirements	Traceability to system requirements

Table 2 Checklist for precision.

SRS Topic	Example
Hardware interfaces	Memory and bus word size consistent with precision
Hardware interfaces	For specific function—see above
Output/input relationships	Explicit statement of precision requirements
Database integrity and accuracy	Must be consistent with above

Table 3 Checklist for functionality.

SRS Topic	Example
System interfaces	Complete definition of the run-time environment
Site adaptation requirements	
Product function (overview)	Traceability to system requirements
Interfaces to other applications	Initialization, synchronization at start-up
User interfaces	Indications and controls for degraded states
Sequence of operations	Recovery from degraded states
Output/input relationships	Completeness of process variables list
Response time requirements	Completeness of parameter descriptions
Data types and hierarchy	Functional completeness of software requirements

Table 4   Checklist for reliability.

SRS Topic	Example
Hardware interfaces Regulatory requirements Redundant operation Reliability requirements	Failure detection capabilities
	Avoidance of single-point failure mechanisms
	Avoidance of correlated failures
	Specification of qualitative and quantitative requirements
Hardware interfaces Software interfaces	Failure modes for specific operations

Table 5   Checklist for robustness.

SRS Topic	Example
System interfaces	Independence of redundant sensors, actuators, and communication channel
Regulatory requirements	Independence of monitors from the monitored function
Redundant operation	Independence of internal processing for redundant processes
Reliability requirements	Specification of minimum acceptable data set
Criticality of the application	Identification of uninterruptible operation
Software interfaces	Independence applied to specific functions
Communication interfaces	Toleration of interruptions and noise
Validity to anomalies	Input-processing requirements
Response to accuracy	Operations requirements
Integrity and accuracy	Limits on step size in outputs
Reliability and availability	Consistency with requirements

Table 6   Checklist for maintainability.

SRS Topic	Example
Hardware requirements	Status monitoring and diagnostics reporting of configuration data
Regulatory requirements	
Redundant operation	Minimum required equipment list
Assumptions and dependencies	Restoration capabilities and times
Hardware interfaces	Status monitoring and diagnostics for specific operations
Effect of parameters	Upgrade and modification support
Maintainability and portability	Consistency with system requirements

Table 7   Checklist for security.

SRS Topic	Example
Hardware interfaces	Physical security
Communication interfaces	Unauthorized access and service interruptions
Regulatory requirements	Consistency with system requirements
Audit functions	Access and operations logs
Hardware interfaces	Prevention of unauthorized parameter changes
Total and simultaneous users	Access control
Security constraints	Consistency with system requirements

Table 8   Checklist for timing.

SRS Topic	Example
Memory constraints	Memory access time
Software interfaces	Consistency with response time requirements, particularly with regard to error checking and rollback
Communication interfaces	
Validity checks on inputs	Evaluation of effect of missed checks on response time
Effect of parameters	Consideration of worst case conditions
Performance requirements	Separate evaluation for each mode of operation
Database frequency of use	Consistency with response requirements

Table 9   Checklist for human–computer interactions.

SRS Topic	Example
Hardware interfaces	Software actions consistent with hardware layout
User interfaces	Event notification feedback on operator inputs
User characteristics	Notification to operator of high-priority events
User interfaces	Event notification for specific tasks

Ten obvious defects of a software product
Kaner and Pels 1998

1. Doesn't do what the publisher's advertisements, manual, or product packaging said it would

2. Doesn't work the way the publisher said it would

3. Crashes

4. Erases or loses your data or introduces errors into it

5. Makes calculation errors

6. Prints reports with errors

7. Gives arguably bad advice (if it is an advice-giving program)

8. Provides information that was erroneous at the time the program was published (if it is an information-giving program)

9. Causes damage to your equipment or physical injury to you

10. Misbehaves in some other way that no reasonable publisher would intend

Ten signs of software project failure
Glass 1999

1. Project managers don't understand users' needs

2. Scope is ill-defined

3. Project changes are managed poorly

4. Chosen technology changes

5. Business needs change

6. Deadlines are unrealistic

7. Users are resistant

8. Sponsorship is lost

9. Project lacks people with appropriate skills

10. Best practices and lessons are ignored

Ten commandments of formal methods
Bowan and Hinchley 1994

1. Thou shall choose the appropriate notation

2. Thou shall formalize, but not overformalize

3. Thou shall estimate costs

4. Thou shall have a formal methods guru on call

5. Thou shall not abandon thy traditional development methods

6. Thou shall document sufficiently

7. Thou shall not compromise thy quality standards

8. Thou shall not be dogmatic

9. Thou shall test, test, and test again

10. Thou shall reuse

Eleven facets of software quality
Arthur 1985

1. Correctness

2. Efficiency

3. Flexibility

4. Integrity

5. Interoperability

6. Maintainability

7. Portability

8. Reliability

9. Reusability

10. Testability

11. Usability

Fifteen software imperfections
Constructed

1. Requirement specification defect

2. Requirement change defect

3. Defect in communication with customer

4. Design defect

5. Logic defect

6. Syntax defect

7. Conformance to standard defect

8. Data defect

9. Control flow defect

10. Interface defect

11. Return code/message defect

12. Help/comment defect

13. Performance improvement defect

14. One-sided decision about deviation from requirements

15. Defective testing

Eighteen key process areas in the CMM
Adapted from SEI 1994

Second Level (repeatable)

1. Requirement management

2. Software project planning

3. Software project tracking and oversight

4. Software subcontract management

5. Software quality assurance

6. Software configuration management

Third Level (defined)

7. Organization process focus

8. Organization process definition

9. Training program

10. Integrated software management

11. Software product engineering

12. Intergroup coordination

13. Peer reviews

Fourth Level (managed)

14. Quantitative process management

15. Software quality management

Fifth Level (optimizing)

16. Defect prevention

17. Technology change management

18. Process change management

Eighteen safety-critical software requirements
From IEEE Std. 1228-1994. Copyright ©1994 IEEE.
All rights reserved.

1. Performance

2. Internal instrumentation

3. Training

4. Completeness

5. Correctness

6. Consistency

7. Testability

8. Robustness

9. Integrity

10. Reliability

11. Usability

12. Flexibility

13. Maintainability

14. Portability

15. Interoperability

16. Accuracy

17. Auditability

18. Security

twenty-two

Twenty-two software quality criteria
Arthur 1985

1. Auditability

2. Accuracy

3. Communication commonality

4. Completeness

5. Complexity

6. Concision

7. Consistency

8. Data commonality

9. Error tolerance

10. Execution efficiency

11. Expandability

12. Generality

13. Hardware independence

14. Instrumentation

15. Modularity

16. Operability

17. Security

18. Self-documentation

19. Simplicity

20. Software system independence

21. Traceability

22. Training

Part Six

Audit and Inspection

Two elements are needed to form a truth—a fact and an abstraction.

—Remy de Gourmont, cited in Brussell 1970

We look at it and don't see it.

—Lao-tzu, sixth century B.C.

One-sentence audit summary
Unknown

Don't forget that your audit report readers are managers. In the summary, the really important findings and observations should be phrased in clear management language, aiming for a one-sentence presentation.

One true sentence
Hemingway 1964

All you have to do is write one true sentence. Write the truest sentence that you know.

One-for-all integrated risk priority number (IRPN)
Adapted from Bluvband and Zilberberg 1998

The risk priority umber (RPN) is the product of O, S, and D (see p. 328). For the unacceptably high RPN, an FMEA team undertakes efforts to reduce the calculated risk through corrective action (CA).

First of all, whenever the severity is catastrophic or very high (see p. 261), the team should pay special attention to the failure cause regardless of the RPN actual value.

On the other hand, when choosing an appropriate CA, especially for not extremely hazardous failure cause, the decision-making must take into account the CA cost (C), effectiveness (E), and interval of time (T) needed for implementation of a "solution." Using the "1 to 10" scale for the values C,

E, and T, in a way similar to the O, S, and D ranking scales, the integrated risk priority number for a given corrective action can be calculated as:

$$IRPN = \frac{(O \times S \times D \times E)}{(C \times T)}$$

Input/output (I/O) first testing
Myers 1979

"I/O first" represents the use of every valid input condition as a test case. Additional input conditions are also used as test cases to demonstrate every valid output.

One way to judge quality
Juran 1989

Quality = (Frequency of deficiencies)/(Opportunity for deficiencies)

Two Vs: verification and validation
Phillips 1998

Verification is "doing it right" and validation is "doing the right one."

1. Verification answers "Did we build the system right?"
2. Validation answers "Did we build the right system?"

Two types of quality characteristics
Common knowledge

1. Variables

2. Attributes

(See also *Three types of data*, p. 210).

——•·•——

Two types of operating characteristic (OC) curves
Bossert 1996

1. *Type A:* A curve showing, for a given sampling plan, the probability of a lot being accepted as a function of the lot quality

2. *Type B:* A curve showing, for a given sampling plan, the probability of a lot being accepted as a function of the process average

——•·•——

Two curves in acceptance sampling
Bossert 1996

1. *Operating characteristic curve:* A curve showing, for a given acceptance control chart configuration, the probability of a process being accepted as a function of the process level

2. *Power curve:* A curve showing the relation between the probability $(1 - \beta)$ of rejecting the hypothesis that a sample belongs to a given population with a given characteristic and the actual population value of that characteristic

Two process characteristics
Bossert 1996

1. *Process capability:* The limits within which a tool or process operates based upon minimum variability as governed by the prevailing circumstances

2. *Process quality:* A statistical measure of the quality of a product of a given process, usually the percentage of nonconforming units in the product

Two possible quality-level protection inputs for sampling planning
Dodge and Romig 1959

1. Average outgoing quality limit (AOQL) protection input

2. Lot tolerance percent defective (LTPD), or limited quality (LQ) input

Remark. Dodge-Romig tables don't use the widespread acceptable quality level (AQL) input, the only one in ANSI/ASQC Z1.4 or MIL Std. 105 E.

Two types of sampling plans using Dodge-Romig tables
Adapted from Dodge and Romig 1959

1. *Single:* Regular sampling, with go/no-go result

2. *Double:* Sampling that is useful when the producer's quality is usually very bad or very good; not effective if the producer's quality is just fair, or "so-so"

Two acceptance control limits (ACLs)
Adapted from Bossert 1996

The action criterion for an acceptance control chart is based on its two acceptance control limits (ACLs). A point that plots outside the ACLs indicates that the process is operating at an undesirable level.

Two phases of defect removal activities
Kan 1995

1. Activities handled directly by the development team (design, reviews, code inspections, unit tests), which for large software projects take place before the code is integrated in the system library

2. Formal tests after code integration

Twofold requirement for audit findings
Common knowledge

1. *Objective:* Not subjective; real

2. *Independent:* Free; self-contained; not governed by someone else; not easily influenced

Remark. Independent is usually objective, because there is no reason to hide or "not discover" something.

Two SEI-distinguished auditlike processes
Adapted from SEI 1997

1. *Assessment:* An "audit" that has the following aims and characteristics:

   a. Process improvement

   b. Assessment of current practice

    c. Input for action plan

    d. Possibility of non-CMM findings

    e. Collaborative style (voluntary disclosure of findings)

    f. Focus on organization

    g. Confidentiality

2. *Evaluation:* An "audit" that has the following aims and characteristics:

    a. Source selection

    b. Evaluation and substantiation of practice

    c. Evaluation of performance risk

    d. CMM findings only

    e. Noncollaborative style ("Discover by yourself whatever you can; we are not interested in disclosing, but we'll answer any question.")

    f. Prediction of next project

Remark. SEI = Software Engineering Institute

Two measures of project timeliness
Adapted from Phillips 1998

1. *Lead:* The difference between the previously announced delivery date and the date on which the new delivery date is announced

2. *Slip:* The difference between the previously announced delivery date and the newly announced one

Two approaches to defect removal effectiveness
Fagan 1976 and Jones 1986

1. Fagan:

$$\frac{\text{Errors found by inspection}}{\text{Total errors in the product before inspection}} \times 100\%$$

2. Jones:

$$\frac{\text{Defects found}}{\text{Defects found + defects not found (i.e. found later)}} \times 100\%$$

 *Remark.* The Fagan approach is a measure of the ability to detect the defect. The Jones expression measures both that ability and the necessity of detection (inspection).

Three groups that fit in one classification
Common knowledge

1. Clearance fits

2. Interference fits

3. Transition fits

Three datum planes at right angles
Common knowledge

1. *Primary datum:* A supporting datum that must be contacted at the three highest points on the surface, which is accomplished by a flat datum-locating surface such as a surface plate

2. *Secondary datum:* An aligning datum that must be contacted at the two highest points on the surface

3. *Tertiary datum:* A stopping datum that must be contacted at the highest point on the surface

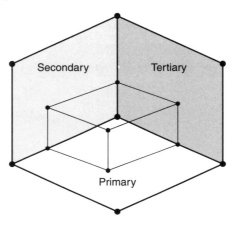

Three test levels
Common knowledge

1. *Integration testing.* Integration testing should not be confused with the testing of integrated objects, which is just higher-level component testing. Integration testing is specifically aimed at exposing the problems that arise from the combination of components.

2. *System testing.* System testing includes testing for performance, security, accountability, configuration sensitivity, start-up, and recovery.

3. *Field testing.* Field testing is sometimes referred to as validation testing.

Three audit types (by the triangle of client, auditor, and supplier)
Common knowledge

1. *First-party:* An internal audit, performed within a company

2. *Second-party:* An audit performed by a customer on a supplier

3. *Third-party:* An audit performed by someone other than the customer on a supplier or regulated entity; for example, an ISO 9000 registration audit

Three types of software examinations (inspections)
Common knowledge

1. *Peer review:* Informal examination of a software element by someone other than the author

2. *Walk-through:* Software element evaluation to detect defects and examine alternatives; a forum for learning and error prevention

3. *Software inspection:* Defect detection and resolution during a prearranged meeting of peers

Three types of field testing
Common knowledge

1. *Acceptance testing:* Formal testing conducted to determine whether a system satisfies its acceptance criteria and to enable the customer to determine whether to accept the system

2. *Qualification testing:* Testing conducted to determine whether a system or component is suitable for operational use

3. *Operational testing:* Testing conducted to evaluate the system or component in its operational environment

Three administrative activities for any anomalous process step

From IEEE Std. 1044-1993. Copyright ©1993 IEEE.
All rights reserved.

1. Recording

2. Classifying

3. Identifying impact

(See also *Four sequential steps of anomalous process classification*, p. 336.)

Three characteristics of failure causes

Adapted from QS 9000, 1995

1. Occurrence

2. Severity

3. Detectability

Remark. Each of the characteristics is estimated on a scale from 1 to 10, with 1 representing the best and 10 the worst.

Three primitive components (multipliers) of the risk priority number (RPN)

Adapted from QS 9000, 1995

1. Occurrence O (1 = improbable, 10 = frequent)

2. Severity S (1 = negligible, 10 = catastrophic)

3. Detectability D (1 = can be detected in an easy and timely manner, 10 = impossible to detect prior to occurrence and influence)

where RPN = $O \times S \times D$ (see also p. 253 and p. 261 for O, S, and D evaluation criteria).

Three measures of system availability
Rau 1970

1. *Point availability:* The probability that the system is in an up state (that is, either operating or operable) at a specified time

2. *Interval availability:* The expected fractional amount of an interval of specified length that the system is in an up state

3. *Inherent availability:* The expected fractional amount of time in a continuum of operating time that the system is in an up state

---

Three elements of an acceptance sampling plan
Common knowledge

1. Sample size or sizes to be used

2. Associated acceptance and rejection criteria

3. Description of the test to be performed on the sample

Three sampling possibilities
Common knowledge

1. Single

2. Double

3. Multiple

Remark. Double sampling and multiple sampling are cost-effective (smaller total sample size) if and only if the supplier's quality is either very high or very low. In the case that the supplier's quality level is "not good enough but not too bad," the total sample size required will usually be higher than that for single sampling.

Three functional parties in any quality audit
Common knowledge

1. *Client:* The party requesting the audit

2. *Auditor:* The party carrying out the audit

3. *Auditee:* The party being audited

Three customers to be satisfied on each audit
Parsowith 1995

1. Auditee

2. Boss

3. Buyer of the service

Three criteria by which you are judged
McCormack 1984

1. Commitment

2. Attention to detail

3. Immediate follow-up

Four key steps to customer satisfaction
Juran and Godfrey 1999

1. Product approval

2. Process review

3. Feedback

4. Continuous improvement, or *kaizen*

Four dispositions used by the material review board
Common knowledge

1. *Use as is:* When will not affect form, fit, function, or interchangeability

2. *Rework:* When can be returned to the original design configuration by specific production action

3. *Repair:* When can be made usable for intended function but will not exactly meet original configuration

4. *Reject:* When is not to be used and is to be scrapped

Four metrics of design quality
Arthur 1985

1. Use of reusable design
2. Module strength and coupling
3. Design readability
4. Design errors

Four elements of managerial support for staff to fulfill new tasks
Unknown

1. Access to time
2. Access to materials
3. Access to equipment
4. Personal support

Four criteria for meeting requirements
Unknown

1. Ability to meet design requirements
2. Controlled process
3. Well-trained and motivated workforce
4. Management support

Four switching procedures
ANSI/ASQ Z1.4 1993

1. *Normal* → *tightened:* When two of five consecutive lots or batches have been rejected on original inspection

2. *Tightened* → *normal:* When five consecutive lots or batches have been considered acceptable on original inspection

3. *Normal* → *reduced:* When all of the following are true:

   • The preceding ten lots or batches have been acceptable.

   • The total number of defectives from the ten lots or batches is equal to or less than an applicable number.

   • Production is at a steady rate.

   • Reduced inspection is considered desirable by the responsible authority.

4. *Reduced* → *normal:* When any one of the following is true:

   • A lot or batch is rejected.

   • The sampling procedure has been terminated without acceptance or rejection under a multiple sampling plan. The lot is considered acceptable but then normal inspection is used.

   • Production becomes irregular or delayed.

   • Other conditions warrant it.

Four phases of an audit
Arter 1994

1. Preparation
2. Performance
3. Reporting
4. Closure

Four elements of the performance phase of an audit
Arter 1994

1. Opening meeting

2. Understanding of the control system

3. Verification of the control system

4. Team and audience meeting

Four-step model for characterizing past performance
Wheeler 2000

1. Identify the critical characteristic and its one-sided product specification

2. Compute a scale factor using a global measure of dispersion

3. Characterize the distance to nearer specification

4. Determine the effective cost production

Four measures used in supplier quality rating plans
Adapted from Juran and Gryna 1993

1. *Product percentage nonconforming:* This is a ratio of the amount of defective items received to the total number of items received

2. *Overall product quality:* This measure summarizes supplier performance at incoming inspection and later phases of product application

3. *Economic analysis:* This type of analysis compares suppliers based on the total dollar cost of specific purchases

4. *Composite plan:* This plan accounts for the fact that supplier performance is not limited to quality: it includes delivery against schedule, price, and other performance categories

Four steps of performance analysis
Unknown

1. Performance measures

2. Current level of performance

3. Target level of performance

4. Impact or reaching target level

Four categories of audit classification
Mills 1988

1. *Why:* The purpose of the audit

2. *What:* The object of the audit

3. *Who:* The nature of the audit

4. *How:* The method of the audit

Four key terms in quality audit sampling
Adapted from Mills 1988

1. *Acceptable performance level (APL).* The acceptable performance level is the lowest performance level that can be considered as acceptable for the function being audited. It is used solely to determine sample size, because the actual performance objective should be 100 percent error-free performance.

2. *Acceptable error rate (AER).* The acceptable error rate is the maximum error rate that can be considered as acceptable for the function being audited: $AER = 1 - APL$.

3. *Confidence level (C).* The confidence level expresses the degree of certainty that the selected sample contains at least one example of each type of error that is present.

4. *Risk (R).* The risk expresses the degree of uncertainty that the selected sample contains at least one example of each type of error that is present: $R = 1 - C$.

Four sequential steps of anomalous process classification

From IEEE Std. 1044-1993. Copyright ©1993 IEEE.
All rights reserved.

1. Recognition

2. Investigation

3. Action

4. Disposition

Four subcontractor qualification factors (per the CMM)

SEI 1997

1. Process capability

2. Professional expertise

3. Application domain knowledge

4. Strategic business alliances

Four ideas detrimental to the quality effort

Russell 1990

1. Volume is always more important than quality

2. Team players tend to get passed over and are easy targets when things are not going well

3. The bigger the better

4. No investment in quality was ever justified

Five questions to ask to determine fitness for use
Juran and Godfrey 1999

1. Who will be the user?

2. How will this product be used?

3. Are there risks to structural integrity, human safety, or the environment?

4. What is the urgency for delivery?

5. How do the alternatives affect the producer's and the user's economics?

Five elements of document evaluation
Common knowledge

1. Purpose of the documents

2. Number of documents produced per time period

3. Time that is necessary for this production

4. Associated cost

5. Standard versus nonstandard documents

Five types of inspection
Adapted from Bossert 1996 and
ASQ's Foundations in Quality 1998

1. Source inspection

2. Receiving inspection

3. In-process inspection

4. Final inspection (component)

5. Final inspection (assembly)

———•———

Five datum planes
Common knowledge

1. Primary (axis)

2. Primary datum (end surface)

3. Secondary (axis)

4. Secondary datum (end surface)

5. Tertiary datum

———•———

Five steps to complete a cause-and-effect study
Unknown

1. Define the problem

2. Draw the problem box and prime arrow

3. Specify the major categories of possible sources contributing to the problem

4. Identify the possible causes associated with each category

5. Analyze the causes and take corrective action

Five generic types of supplier-rating systems
Adapted from Bhote 1989

1. *No rating:* The rationale is that purchasing and quality departments know which companies are good and bad; therefore, a formal rating system is not needed.

2. *Quality rating only:* This type of rating is based on incoming inspection statistics.

3. *Quality and delivery rating (A):* This graphic method charts the quality rating against the delivery rating. Suppliers can also be grouped into A, B, C, or NR (not rated) categories.

4. *Quality and delivery rating (B):* This cost index method of rating is based on a fixed dollar penalty for nonconformances.

5. *Comprehensive method:* This method measures and rates agreed-on variables such as quality, cost, delivery, service, and so on, with weights applied.

Five steps of effective interviewing
Phillips 1998

1. Prepare

2. Introduce

3. Interview

4. Close

5. Follow up

Five special participant roles during the software inspection process
Gilb and Graham 1993

1. *Checker (inspector):* Checks for issues, using rules

2. *Scribe (checker):* Writes the issues and other items during the logging meeting

3. *Role specialist:* Serves as a checker who has undertaken specific checking tasks

4. *Moderator:* Acts as the inspection leader

5. *Author:* Checks that logging is intelligible during the logging meeting

Six shipping errors
Constructed

1. Wrong quantity

2. Wrong product

3. Wrong packaging

4. Wrong address

5. Wrong pricing

6. Wrong timing

Six elements of the true cost of purchased material
Constructed

1. Cost of incoming inspection

2. Cost of material review

3. Cost of contact vendor

4. Cost of production problems/delays

5. Cost of extra inventory

6. Cost of customer complaints

Six requisites for reliable estimation procedures
Adapted from Park 1996a

1. A corporate memory (historical database)

2. Structured processes for estimating product size and reuse

3. Mechanisms for extrapolating from demonstrated accomplishments of past projects

4. Audit trails (recording and explanation of the values for the cost model parameters that are used to produce each estimate)

5. Integrity in dealing with dictated costs and schedules (following of legitimate design-to-cost or build-to-cost processes so that imposed answers are acceptable)

6. Data collection and feedback processes that foster capturing and correctly interpreting data from work performed

Six techniques for determining the cost of poor quality
Unknown

1. Collection of cost data by account

2. Collection of cost data by aggregation of employees' work hours

3. Collection of labor cost data by project

4. Estimation of cost data based on the percentage of defects

5. Estimation of cost data based on the number of occurrences of a poor quality event

6. Collection of cost data based on interviews and surveys

Six incoming inspection types
Adapted from Bossert 1996 and
ASQ's Foundations in Quality 1998

1. *Inspection, 100%.* This inspection of all the units in a lot or batch involves the removal or replacement of units not accepted during inspection.

2. *Inspection, curtailed.* In this type of sampling scheme, inspection of the sample is stopped as soon as a decision is certain.

3. *Inspection, normal.* This type of inspection, which utilizes an acceptance sampling scheme, applies when a process is considered to be operating at its acceptable quality level or at a slightly higher level.

4. *Inspection, reduced.* This sampling scheme allows the use of sample sizes that are smaller than those used in normal inspection. Reduced inspection is used as the sampling scheme in instances where there is adequate experience with the submitted quality level and other stated conditions apply.

5. *Inspection, rectifying.* This type of inspection involves the removal or replacement of variant units during inspection of all the units, or of some specified number, in a lot or batch that was not accepted by acceptance sampling.

6. *Inspection, tightened.* This sampling scheme applies stricter acceptance criteria than those applied under normal inspection. Tightened inspection is used in some sampling schemes as a protective measure to increase the probability of rejecting lots when experience has shown that the level of submitted quality has deteriorated significantly.

Seven key issues of controls
Hines et al. 2000

1. Environmental

2. Employee

3. Buffering

4. Quality

5. Cost

6. Delivery

7. Availability and performance efficiency

The seven most popular published statistical sampling tables
Common knowledge

1. Dodge-Romig tables

2. MIL Std. 105D, ANSI/ASQC Z1.4, and ISO 2859 (all essentially similar)

3. Sequential plans

4. Continuous sampling plans

5. Chain sampling and skip-lot plans

6. Columbia sampling tables

7. Zero acceptance number (C = 0) sampling plans

Eight steps to building a balanced scorecard
Kaplan and Norton 1993

1. The scope of the balanced scorecard is defined

2. A facilitator gathers information for the scorecard through interviews with senior management

3. The facilitator distributes the information at an executive workshop designated to develop a rough draft of the measures for a balanced scorecard

4. The facilitator generates a new report and a rough draft scorecard

5. A second workshop is held with senior management and additional levels of management. The draft is refined and objectives provided for the proposed measures

6. A third workshop finalizes the vision, objectives, and measures

7. A new task team develops an implementation plan

8. Periodic reviews of the balanced scorecard are conducted.

Eight basic designs for testing training effectiveness
Adapted from Campbell and Stanley 1963

1. *One-shot case study design.* A treatment (training or simulation) T is applied to a group and some effect (observation) O is measured:

   T   O

2. *One-group pretest–posttest design.* A measurement is made before the treatment is applied, followed by another test:

O   T   O

3. *Pretest–posttest control group design.* A randomized control group R (without the treatment) is included:

R   O   T   O

R   O   O

4. *Time series experiment design.* The treatment is applied after a series of measurements, and then follow-up measurements are applied to detect differences:

O   O   O   O   T   O   O   O   O

5. *Nonequivalent group design.* This is similar to the pretest–posttest control group design, but the selection of the group N is not randomized (N refers to "nonequivalent"):

N   O   T   O

N   O   O

6. *Regression discontinuity design.* This design is a pretest–posttest two-group method (C is the cutoff point):

C   O   T   O

C   O   O

7. *Regression point displacement design.* Two groups participate:

   • A control group

   • The group of interest

   The difference between the groups is significant when the amount of deviation from the point in question is statistically significant.

8. *Proxy pretest.* The pretest is conducted after the program or treatment has been applied:

N   O   T   O

N   O   O

Nine steps of the audit preparation phase
Arter 1994

1. Define the purpose of the audit

2. Define the scope of the audit

3. Determine the resources to be applied

4. Identify the authority for the audit

5. Identify the performance standard to be used

6. Contact the auditee

7. Develop written checklists of the data needs

8. Review the performance history of the auditee

9. Develop an initial understanding of the control systems

Nine audit types
Constructed

1. *Internal audit:* An audit performed by a company upon its own system, procedures, and facilities

2. *External audit:* An audit performed by a company upon its own suppliers or subsuppliers

3. *Extrinsic audit:* A management audit performed either by a customer or by a regulatory body or inspection agency (or their representative)

4. *System audit:* A review of the quality system

5. *Process audit:* An audit of in-process controls of operations

6. *Product audit:* Reinspection of a product (may be physical or functional)

7. *Compliance audit:* An audit that asks whether the defined management system is being implemented

8. *Follow-up audit:* An audit performed to verify and assess the efficacy of corrective action taken as a result of a previous audit finding

9. *Survey:* A comprehensive (usually pre-award) evaluation that analyzes facilities, technical capability, economic stability, personnel, resources, and so on, as well as the quality system

Ten quality success measures
Unknown

1. External customer satisfaction

2. Internal customer satisfaction

3. Training and development

4. On-time performance

5. Quality of orders

6. Warranty and deficiency

7. Availability and forced outage

8. Accounts receivable

9. Cost of nonconformance

10. Cash conversion efficiency

Ten types of technical review
MIL Std. 1521B 1985

1. System requirement review (SRR)

2. System design review (SDR)

3. Software specification review (SSR)

4. Preliminary design review (PDR)

5. Critical design review (CDR)

6. Test readiness review (TRR)

7. Functional configuration audit (FCA)

8. Physical configuration audit (PCA)

9. Formal qualification review (FQR)

10. Production readiness review (PRR)

seventeen

Seventeen software plan documents, reviews, and audits
From appendixes to IEEE Std. 1028-1988.

1. *Software requirement specification (SRS).* The SRS documents the essential requirements of the software and its external interfaces.

2. *Software requirement review (SRR).* The SRR is held to ensure the adequacy of the requirements stated in the SRS.

3. *Software verification and validation plan (SVVP).* The SVVP identifies and describes the methods to be used.

4. *Software verification and validation plan review (SVVPR).* The SVVPR is held to evaluate the adequacy and completeness of the verification and validation methods defined in the SVVP.

5. *Software verification and validation report (SVVR).* The SVVR describes the results of the execution of the SVVP.

6. *Software design description (SDD).* This representation of software is created to facilitate analysis, planning, implementation, and decision making.

7. *Software quality assurance (SQA).* The SQA is a planned and systematic pattern of all actions necessary to provide adequate confidence that an item or product conforms to established technical requirements.

8. *Software quality assurance plan (SQAP).* The SQAP is a document that delineates the management actions, controls and responsibilities required for the SQA function.

9. *Critical design review (CDR).* This review is conducted to verify that the detailed design of one or more configuration items satisfies special requirements.

10. *Preliminary design review (PDR).* The PDR is conducted to evaluate the progress, technical adequacy, and risk resolution of the selected design approach for one or more selection items.

11. *Software configuration management plan (SCMP).* The SCMP documents methods to be used for identifying software items, controlling and implementing changes, and recording and reporting change implementation status.

12. *Software configuration management plan review (SCMPR).* The SCMPR is held to evaluate the adequacy and completeness of the configuration management methods defined in the SCMP.

13. *User documentation review (UDR).* This review is held to evaluate the adequacy of user documentation.

14. *Functional audit (FA).* This audit is held prior to software delivery to verify that all requirements specified in the SRS have been met.

15. *Physical audit (PA).* This audit is held to verify that the software and its documentation are internally consistent and are ready for delivery.

16. *In-process audit (IPA).* The IPA is held to verify the consistency of the design.

17. *Managerial review (MR).* Managerial reviews are held periodically to assess the execution of all the actions and the items identified in the SQAP. These reviews are held by an organizational element independent of the unit being reviewed or by a qualified third party.

Twenty activities that answer the question "Is it OK?"
Constructed

1. Accreditation:

   • The procedure for recognizing both the technical competence and the impartiality of a test laboratory to carry out its associated tasks (UK DTI, ITSEC, 1991)

   • The procedure for accepting an information technology system for use within a particular environment

2. Analysis:

   • The determination of the essential qualities, performance, and limitations of an item by cognitive or computational methods (ESA, ECSS-P-001A, 1997)

3. Appraisal:

- The conducting of inspections, tests, and other planned evaluations to ensure that requirements are met (MIL Std. 109C, 1994)

4. Approval:

- Permission for a product, process, or service to be marketed or used for stated purposes or under stated conditions (ISO/IEC, Guide 2, 1996)

- Formal agreement to use or apply an item (ESA, ECSS-P-001a, 1997)

5. Assessment:

- The result of a systematic examination and judgment of something against stated criteria or requirements (BSI, BS 4778-3.1, 1991)

6. Audit:

- A systematic and independent examination to determine whether the procedures specific to the requirements of a product comply with the planned arrangements, are implemented effectively, and are suitable to achieve the specified objectives (CENELEC, prEN50126, 1998)

- A systematic and independent examination to determine whether quality activities and related results comply with planned arrangements and whether these arrangements are implemented effectively and are suitable to achieve objectives (ISO 8402-1986)

- A human evaluation process to determine the degree of adherence to prescribed norms (criteria, standards) and resulting in a judgment (CAN-CSA-Q395-1981)

- Examination for the purpose of understanding (IEEE Std.1074-1991)

Remark. Discovery finding is a special type of audit. The audit is based on zero-acceptance statistical sampling plan. Zero defects in the sample will allow one to guaranty with the required confidence level (for example, 90%) that the given percentage of the entire population (lets say, 99%) is failure free.

7. Certification:

- The procedure by which a third party gives written assurance that a product, process, or service conforms to specified requirements (ISO/IEC, Guide 2, 1996)

8. Check, checkout:

   - The test carried out before the system is put into commission (Holcher and Rader 1986)

   - Tests or observations of an item to determine its condition or status (MIL Std. 721C, 1981)

9. Demonstration:

   - A dynamic analysis technique that relies on observation of system or component behavior during execution, without the need for postexecution analysis, to detect errors, violations of development standards, and other problems (IEEE Std. 610.12-1990)

10. Diagnosis:

    - The action of determining the cause of an error in location and nature (Laprie 1992)

11. Evaluation:

    - The process of defining whether an item or activity meets specified criteria (MIL Std. 2167A, 1988)

    - Determination of fitness for use (IEEE Std. 1074-1991)

Remark. An example is the risk evaluation process, in which judgments are made on the tolerability of the risk on the basis of risk analysis, taking into account factors such as socioeconomic and environmental aspects (IEC 300-3-9-1995).

12. Examination:

    - An element of inspection consisting of investigation, without the use of special laboratory appliances, of procedures, supplies, or services to determine conformance to those specified requirements that can be determined by the investigation (MIL Std. 109C, 1994)

    - A spoken or written test of knowledge as a final acceptance activity for professional certification or diploma

13. Inspection:

    - Conformity evaluation by observational judgment accompanied as appropriate by measurement, testing, or gauging (ISO/IEC Guide 2, 1996)

14. Qualification:

    - The process of determining whether a system or component is suitable for operational use (IEEE Std. 610.12-1990)

15. Review:

    - A process or meeting during which a work product, or set of work products, is presented to project personnel, managers, users, customers, or other interested parties for comment or approval (IEEE Std. 610-12-1990; IEEE Std. 1058.1-1988)

    - Systematic examination of items for the purpose of assessing the results obtained at a given time in the project, by persons not themselves responsible for the project (ESA, ECSS-P-001A, 1997)

    - An evaluation of software element(s) or project status to ascertain discrepancies from planned results and to recommend improvement; follows a formal process (IEEE Std. 1028-1988)

Remark. Design review—A formal and independent examination of an existing or proposed design for the purpose of detection and remedy of deficiencies in the requirements and design that could affect such things as reliability, performance, maintainability performance, maintenance support performance requirements, and fitness for purpose, as well as for the identification of potential improvements (UK MoD Def. Std. 00-49, 1996)

16. Surveillance:

    - The observation of particular activities being performed as part of a production or verification process in order to validate the actions being taken, the results noted, and the decisions being made

    - The continuing evaluation, analysis, and verification of a supplier's records, methods, procedures, products, and services in order to ensure that requirements are met (CAN-CSA-Z299.1 through CAN-CSA-Z299.4, 1985 editions, titled "Quality Assurance Program Requirements," Categories 1 through 4)

    - Monitoring or observation to verify whether an item or activity conforms to specified requirements (ANSI/ASQC A3-1987)

17. Test:

    - The formal process of exercising or putting to trial a system or item by manual or automatic means to identify differences between specified, expected, and actual results (ESA, ECSS-P-001A, 1997)

    - Technical operation that consists of the determination of one or more characteristics of a given product, process, or service according to a specified procedure (ISO/IEC, Guide 2, 1996)

    - An activity performed in order to ensure that a given product functions correctly (in a defined stressful environment during a defined time)

18. Validation:

    - The process of determining that the requirements are the right requirements and that they are complete (RTCA, DO178B, 1992)

    - The process of evaluating software at the end of the software development process to ensure compliance with software requirements (UK MoD, Def. Std. 00-55, 1997; IEEE Std. 729-1983)

19. Verification:

    - The process of evaluating a system or component to determine whether the products of a given development phase satisfy the conditions imposed at the start of that phase

    - Formal proof of program correctness (IEEE Std. 610.12-1990)

20. Walk-through:

    - A static analysis technique in which a designer or programmer leads members of the development team and other interested parties through a segment of documentation or code, and the participants ask questions and make comments about possible errors, violations of development standards, and other problems (adapted from Gilb and Graham 1993).

magic numbers and percentages

360° feedback process
Common knowledge

This methodology evaluates performance using self, peers, subordinates, assistants, management, different customers (internal and external), and suppliers.

5% producer's risk
Common knowledge

The degree of producer's risk (the risk that, through a sampling plan, a good lot will be rejected by a customer) is typically 5%.

85%–99% working range
Common knowledge

The acceptance probability P_a for a single sampling plan in ANSI Z1.4 (MIL Std. 105) ranges from 85% to 99%, that is, not always 95% (not 5% producer's risk), what both parties (supplier and customer) usually are assuming using the sampling procedures.

5% rule
Common knowledge

Most companies spend a small portion, only 5%, of their time figuring out what went wrong.

------·-·------

25–30 rule
Common knowledge

The number of questions in a survey questionnaire should range from 25 to 30 in order to be adequate.

References

AFSC/AFLC 00-45. 1988. Department of the Air Force, Headquarters Air
    Force Systems Command, Andrews Air Force Base DC 20334-5000
    Headquarters Air Force Logistics Command, Wright-Patterson Air Force
    Base OH 45433-5001, Software risk abatement, AFSC/AFLC Pamphlet
    00-45, 30 September 1988.

Adams, S. 1996. *The Dilbert Pinciple.* New York: HarperCollins.

Albrecht, K. 1992. *The Only Thing that Matters.* New York: HarperCollins.

Altshuller, G. S. 1998. *Forty Principles: TRIZ Keys to Technical Innovation.*
    Worcester, MA: Technical Innovation Center.

AMSC no. F3631. HQ U.S. Air force, Washington, DC: Department of Defense.

ANSI/ASQC A1-1978. 1978. *Definitions, Symbols, Formulas, and Tables for
    Control Charts.* Milwaukee: ASQC Quality Press.

ANSI/ASQC A2-1978. 1978. *Quality Systems Terminology.* Milwaukee: ASQC
    Quality Press.

ANSI/ASQC A2-1978. 1978. *Terms, Symbols, and Definitions for Acceptance
    Sampling.* Milwaukee: ASQC Quality Press.

ANSI/ASQC A3-1987. 1987. *Quality System Terminology.* Milwaukee: ASQC
    Quality Press.

ANSI/ASQC Z1.4-1993. 1993. *Sampling Procedures and Tables for Inspection by
    Attributes.* Milwaukee: ASQC Quality Press.

Arkin, H. 1984. *Handbook of Sampling for Auditing and Accounting.* 3rd ed.
    Englewood Cliffs, NJ: Prentice Hall.

Arter, D. R. 1994. *Quality Audits for Improved Performance.* 2nd ed. Milwaukee:
    ASQC Quality Press.

Arthur, L. J. 1985. *Measuring Programmer Productivity and Software Quality.*
    New York: John Wiley & Sons.

ASSE. 1988. *The Dictionary of Terms Used in the Safety Profession.* 3rd ed.
    American Society of Safety Engineers.

ASQ's Foundations in Quality. 1998. *Certified Quality Manager.* Milwaukee: ASQC Quality Press.

ASQ's Foundations in Quality Learning Series. 2001. *Certified Quality Manager.* Milwaukee: ASQC Quality Press.

ASQC Chemical and Process Industries Division, Chemical Interest Committee. 1987. *Quality Assurance for the Chemical and Process Industries: A Manual of Good Practices.* Milwaukee: ASQC Quality Press.

ASTM Committee E-11. 1972. Proposed revision to ASTM E456-72, *Terminology for Statistical Methods.* Philadelphia: American Society for Testing and Materials.

Atkinson, H., J. Hamburg, and C. Ittner. 1994. *Linking Quality to Profits: Quality-Based Cost Management.* Milwaukee: ASQC Quality Press.

Augustine, N. 1987. *Augustine's Laws,* New York: Penguin Books.

Baker, S., and K. Baker. 1998. *The Complete Idiot's Guide to Project Management.* New York: Alpha Books.

Barel, A. 1991. Discussion at the management meeting at ALD, November 14.

Bechtell, M. 1995. *The Management Compass: Steering the Corporation Using Hoshin Planning.* New York: AMA Management Briefing Division.

Beckenbach, E. F., and R. Bellman. 1961. *Inequalities.* Berlin: Springer-Verlag.

Bell, R. 1994. *Customers As Partners: Building Relationships that Last.* San Francisco: Berrett-Koehler.

Bensley, F. A., and B. L. Wortman. 1995. *ISO Primer.* 2nd ed. Terre Haute: Quality Council of Indiana.

Bhote, K. R. 1988. *World Class Quality: Design of Experiments Made Easier, More Cost Effective than SPC.* New York: AMA Membership Publication Division.

————. 1989. *Strategic Supply Management.* New York: Amacom.

————. 1996. *Beyond Customer Satisfaction to Customer Loyalty: The Key to Greater Profitability.* New York: AMA Membership Publication Division.

Birsner, E. P., and R. D. Balsley. 1982. *Practical Guide to Customer Service Management and Operations.* New York: Amacom.

Blanchard, B. S. 1986. *Logistics Engineering and Management.* 3rd ed. Upper Saddle River, NJ: Prentice Hall.

Blum, B. 1992. *Software Engineering: A Holistic View.* Oxford: Oxford University Press.

Bluvband, M. 1968. Conversation of the author's father Max Bluvband with the author.

Bluvband, Z. 1995. "Quality Breakdown Structure: New Technology for Quality Assessment." *Proceedings of the 39th EOQ Annual Congress. June 12–15, 1995, vol. 3.* Lausanne: SAQ Swiss Association for the Promotion of Quality.

————. 1996a. Integrated Quality and Logistics Management (IQLM). Tutorial presented at the 12th International Logistics Congress. Athens, Greece. September 27–29.

————. 1996b. "Qualimetry: A Constructive Approach to Quality Improvement." *Quality Observer* 5, no. 8.

————. 1997. *Multisensitive LCC Analysis with Estimates.* Jerusalem: Proceedings of the 13th International Logistics Congress, September 17–19, 1997.

————. 1997b. Risk Management. Tutorial at the 13th SOLE International Logistics Congress. Jerusalem. September 17–19.

————. 1998. Keynote speech at the 12 International ISQ Conference. Jerusalem. December 1.

————. 1999a. Keynote speech at the National ISQ Conference. Haifa. November 24–25.

————. 1999b. Total Ownership Cost. Tutorial at Mid-Atlantic Logistics SOLE Conference. Hampton, VA. April 23–24.

————. 2000. *Organizational Management and Control through the Taguchi Approach of Robust Design.* Jerusalem: Proceedings of the Millennium International Conference of the Israel Society for Quality, November 28–30, 2000, vol. II, ISAS International Seminars, P.O. Box 34001, Jerusalem 91340, Israel.

————. 2001. Software Reliability and Availability. Course presented at IsraStar conference. Tel Aviv. October 18.

————. 2002. Reliability-Centered Software Test Planning. RAMS. Seattle, WA. January 28–31.

Bluvband, Z., and P. Grabov. 1996. Integrated Process Control and Engineering. 50th AQC Proceedings. Chicago, IL. May 13–15.

————. 1998. *Advanced SPC Techniques for Process Yield Improvement Tutorial.* San Francisco: Course presented at Semicon West 98, July, 1998.

Bluvband, Z., and E. Zilberberg. 1998. Knowledge Base Approach to Integrated FMEA. ASQ's 52nd Annual Quality Congress Proceedings. Philadephia, PA: May 4–6.

Boehm, B. 1989. *Software Risk Management.* Los Alamitos, CA: IEEE CS Press.

Boehm, B. 1996. "Anchoring the Software Process." *IEEE Software* 13, no 4.

Bogan, C., and M. English. 1994. *Benchmarking for Best Practices: Winning through Innovative Adaptation.* New York: McGraw-Hill.

Bossert, J. L., ed. 1996. *Glossary and Tables for Statistical Quality Control,* Third Edition. Milwaukee: ASQC Quality Press.

Bossert, J. L., ed. 1988. *Procurement Quality Control.* 4th ed. Milwaukee: ASQC Quality Press.

Bowan, J. P., and M. G. Hinchley. 1994. *Ten Commandments of Formal Methods.* Technical Report no. 350. Cambridge: University of Cambridge Computer Laboratory.

Braude, J. M. 1992. *Complete Speaker's and Toastmaster's Library.* 2nd ed. Englewood Cliffs, NJ: Prentice Hall.

Bredrup, H., and R. Bredrup. 1995. *Performance Measurement to Support Continuous Improvement of Customer Satisfaction.* Lausanne, Switzerland: Proceedings of the 39th EOQ Annual Congress, vol. 1, June 13, 1995.

Brooks, F. 1975. *The Mythical Man Month.* Reading, MA: Addison Wesley.

Brussell, E. E. 1970. *Dictionary of Quotable Definitions.* Englewood Cliffs, NJ: Prentice Hall.

British Standards Institution. BS 4778, Part 1, *Quality Vocabulary–International Terms,* 1991.

British Standards Institution. BS 4778, Part 2, *Quality Concepts and Related Definitions,* 1991.

British Standards Institution, BS 4778, Part 3, *Availability, Reliability and Maintainability Terms*; Section 3.1: "Guide to concepts and related definitions," 1991.

British Standards Institution, BS 4778, Part 3, *Availability, Reliability and Maintainability Terms*; Section 3.2: "Glossary of international terms," 1991 (equal to IEC 50-191, 1990).

Bulmer, M. G. 1967. *Principles of Statistics.* London: Oliver & Boyd.

Campbell, D., and J. Stanley. 1963. *Experimental and Quasi-Experimental Designs for Research.* Chicago: Rand McNally.

CAN-CSA-Q395-1981. Quality audits (Appendix 1A.3.1.2) CAN-CSA-Z299.1 through CAN-CSA-Z299.4, 1981 editions, titled *Quality assurance program requirements,* categories 1 through 4.

CCPS, 1993. Center for Chemical Process Safety of the American Institute of Chemical Engineers, *Guidelines for safe automation of chemical processes.* New York: 1993. Copyright (1992) by the American Institute of Chemical Engineers and reproduced by permission of Center for Chemical Process Safety of AIChE.

CEN, EN 298. 1993. European Committee for Standardization, EN 298, *Automatic Gas Burner Control Systems for Gas Burners and Gas Burning Appliances with or without Fans.*

CENELEC, prEN50126. 1998. *Railway Applications: The Specification and Demonstration of Reliability, Availability, Maintainability and Safety* (RAMS).

CENELEC, ENV50129. 1998. *Railway Applications: Safety Related Electronic Systems for Signaling.*

Cheung, W. H., J. P. Black, and P. A. Manning. 1990. "Framework for Distributed Debugging." *IEEE Software* (January).

Coallier, F., R. McKenzie, J. Wilson, and J. Hatz. 1994. *Trillium, a Model for Telecom Product Development and Support Process Capability,* Release 3.0. Canada: Bell (December 1994).

Collins, B., and E. Huge. 1993. *Management by Policy: How Companies Focus Their Total Quality Efforts to Achieve Competitive Advantage.* Milwaukee: ASQC Quality Press.

Constantine, L. L. 1993. "Work Organization: Paradigms for Project Management and Organization." *Communications of the ACM* (Association for Computer Machinery) 36, no. 10.

Cortada, J. W., and J. A. Woods. 1995. *The McGraw-Hill Encyclopedia of Quality Terms and Concepts.* New York: McGraw-Hill.

Covey, S. R. 1989. *The Seven Habits of Highly Effective People.* New York: Simon & Schuster.

———. 1991. *Principle-Centered Leadership.* New York: Summit Books.

Covey, S. R., A. R. Merril, and R. R. Merril. 1994. *First Things First.* New York: Covey Leadership Center.

Cox, J., J. Blackstone, and M. Spencer, eds. 1995. *APICS Dictionary.* 8th ed. Falls Church, VA: American Production and Inventory Control Society.

Crosby, P. B. 1980. *Quality Is Free.* New York: McGraw-Hill.

———. 1996. *The Absolutes of Leadership.* San Francisco: Jossey-Bass.

Crow, E., F. A. Davis, and M. W. Maxfield. 1960. *Statistics Manual.* New York: Dover Publications.

CSA International, CAN/CSA-Q396.1.1, *Quality Assurance Program for the Development of Software Used in Critical Applications,* 1989.

D'Avenie, R. A. 1995. "Coping with Hyper-Competition: Utilizing the New 7S's Framework." *Academy of Management Executives* 9, no. 3.

Day, R. G. 1993. *Quality Function Deployment: Linking a Company with Its Customers.* Milwaukee: ASQC Quality Press.

De Bono, E. 1990. *Lateral Thinking: Creativity Step-by-Step.* New York: HarperCollins.

Del Vecchio, R. J. 1997. *Understanding Design of Experiments: A Primer for Technologists.* Munich: Hanser Publishers.

Delavigne, K. T., and J. D. Robertson. 1994. *Deming's Profound Changes: When Will the Sleeping Giant Awaken?* Englewood Cliffs, NJ: Prentice Hall.

Deming, W. E. 1994. *The New Economics for Industry, Government, Education.* 2nd ed. Cambridge: Massachusetts Institute of Technology.

———. 1997. *Out of the Crisis.* Cambridge: W. Edwards Deming Institute, Massachusetts Institute of Technology.

Denton, D., and C. Boyd. 1994. *Did You Know? Fascinating Facts and Fallacies about Business.* Englewood Cliffs, NJ: Prentice Hall.

Deutsches Institut fur Normung, DIN-V-VDE 0801, Principles for computers in safety-related systems, 1990.

Dobbins, R. D. 1995. "A Failure of Methods, Not Philosophy." *Quality Progress* 28, no. 7 (July 1995).

Dodge, H., and H. Romig. 1959. *Sampling Inspection Tables.* 2nd ed. New York: John Wiley & Sons.

Driver, M. J., K. R. Brousseau, and P. L. Hunsaker. 1993. *The Dynamic Decision Maker.* San Francisco: Jossey-Bass.

ECSS-P-001A. European Space Agency. *Glossary of Terms,* Rev. 1, 1997.

EFQM Web site: www.qpronline.com/EFQM.

Ehrlich, E., and G. R. Hawes. 1984. *Speak for Success: The No-Fear Guide to Speaking Anywhere, Anytime, to Anyone.* New York: Bantam Books.

Fagan, M. E. 1976. "Design and Code Inspections to Reduce Errors in Program Development." *IBM Systems Journal* 15, no. 3.

Feigenbaum, A. V. 1961. *Total Quality Control.* New York: McGraw Hill.

———. 1983. *Total Quality Control.* 3rd ed. New York: McGraw-Hill.

Fisher, D. 1995. *The Just-in-Time Self Test: Success through Assessment and Implementation.* Burr Ridge Parkway: Richard D. Irwin.

Ford Motor Company. 1999. *Training Manual for the G-8D Process.* www.triz-journal.com/archives/2000/07/c.

Fragola, J. R. 1996. Human Reliability Analysis. Rev. 04. Jerusalem Tutorial, 11th International Conference of the ISQ. November 4.

Fuqua, N. B. 1987. *Reliability Engineering for Electronic Design.* New York: Marcel Dekker.

Furlong, C. 1993. *Marketing for Keeps: Building Your Business by Retaining Your Customers.* New York: John Wiley & Sons.

Gale, B. T., with R. C. Wood. 1994. *Managing Customer Value: Creating Quality and Service that Customers Can See.* New York: The Free Press.

Galin, D., and Z. Bluvband. 1995. *Software Quality Assurance.* Tel-Aviv: Opus.

Garvin, D. A. 1988. *Managing Quality: The Strategic and Competitive Edge.* New York: The Free Press.

Gause, D. C., and G. M. Weinberg. 1989. *Exploring Requirements: Quality before Design.* New York: Dorset House.

Geddes, L. 1993. *Through the Customer's Eyes.* New York: Amacom.

Gibbs Group Web site. gibbsgroup.com/inventors_cafe/fraud.html .

Gilb, T., and D. Graham. 1993. *Software Inspection.* Edinburgh Gate Harlow, England: Addison Wesley Longman.

Glass, R. 1999. *Computing Calamities: Lessons Learned from Products and Companies that Failed.* Upper Saddle River, NJ: Prentice Hall.

Glichev, A. V. et al. 1970. Qualimetry. (In Russian). *Standards and Quality* no. 11.

GOAL/QPC Research Committee. 1991. *Quality Function Deployment Advanced QFD Application Articles*, Research Report no. 90-12-03. GOAL/QPC: Methuen, MA.

Goldratt, E. 1990. *Theory of Constraints.* Great Barrington, MA: North River Press.

Grabov, P. 1998. Letter to author. July 15.

Grey, S. 1995. *Practical Risk Assessment for Project Management.* Chichester, West Sussex, England: John Wiley & Sons.

Hammer, M., and J. Champy. 1994. *Reengineering the Corporations.* New York: HarperCollins.

Hardjono, T. W., S. ten Have, and W. D. ten Have. 2000. *The European Way to Excellence.* Oxford, England: European Quality Publications.

Harrington, H. J., E. K. C. Esseling, and K. C. Harm van Nimwegen. 1997. *Business Process Improvement Workbook Documentation: Analysis, Design, and Management of Business Process Improvement.* New York: McGraw-Hill.

Harris, A. B., and T. A. Harris. 1985. *Staying OK.* New York: Harper & Row.

Harry, M. J., and R. Schroeder. 1999. *Six Sigma: The Breakthrough Management Strategy Revolutionizing the World's Top Corporations.* New York: Doubleday.

Hartman, B. 1983. "Implementing Quality Improvement." *The Juran Report,* no 2 (November).

Hayes, B. E. 1991. *Measuring Customer Satisfaction: Development and Use of Questionnaires.* Milwaukee: ASQC Quality Press.

Hayslip, W. R. 1994. "Measuring Customer Satisfaction in Business Markets." *Quality Progress* 27, no. 4 (April 1994).

Hecht, M., and H. Hecht. 2001a. Digital Systems Software Requirements Guidelines: Failure Descriptions. *SoHaR, NUREG/CR-6734.*

———. 2001b. Digital Systems Software Requirements Guidelines: Guidelines. *SoHaR, NUREG/CR-6734.*

Hemingway, E. 1964. *A Moveable Feast.* New York: Collier Books.

Hersey, P., and K. Blanchard. 1982. *Management of Organizational Behavior Utilizing Human Resources.* 4th ed. Englewood Cliffs, NJ: Prentice Hall.

Heskett, J. L., T. O. Jones, G. W. Loveman, et al. 1994. "Putting the Service-Profit Chain to Work." *Harvard Business Review* (March–April).

Hesse, H. 1951. *Siddhartha.* New York: New Directions.

Hetzel, B. 1993. *Making Software Measurement Work.* New York: John Wiley & Sons.

Higuera, R. P. 1995. *Team Risk Management: CrossTalk.* Washington, DC: U.S. Dept. of Defense.

Hildebrand, D. K., and L. Ott. 1991. *Statistical Thinking for Managers.* 3rd ed. Belmont, CA: Duxbury Press.

Hines, P., R. Lamming, D. Jones, P. Cousins, and N. Rich. 2000. *Value Stream Management: Strategy and Excellence in the Supply Chain.* London: Financial Times Prentice Hall.

Holscher, H., and R. Rader. 1986. *Microcomputers in Safety Technique: An Aid to Orientation for Developer and Manufacturer.* Bayern: Verlag TUV.

Hornby, A. S., ed. 1989. *Oxford Advanced Learner's Dictionary of Current English.* 4th ed. London: Oxford University Press.

HSE. 1991. *Software for Computers in Safety Related Applications.* London: Health and Safety Executive.

Huck, S., and W. Cormier. 1996. *Reading Statistics and Research.* 2nd ed. New York: HarperCollins.

Humphrey, W. 1995. *A Discipline for Software Engineering.* Reading, MA: Addison Wesley.

IBM MHVPL PTM Work Group. 1990. *Requirements for Program Trouble Memoranda.* Wappingers Falls, NY: IBM Mid Hudson Valley Programming Lab.

IEC 300-3-9. 1995. "Risk Analysis of Technological Systems." *Dependability Management*, Part 3, Application guide, Section 9.

IEC 902. 1987. Industrial Process Measurement and Control: Terms and Definitions.

IEC 1131-1. 1992. Programmable Controllers; Part 1, "General Information."

IEC Std. 60300-1/Ed 2. 2001. *Dependability Management—Part 1: Dependability Programme Management.*

IEC Std. 60300-2.2001. Dependability management—Part 2: Guidance for dependability programme management.

IEC 61508. 1998. Functional Safety of Electrical/Electronic/Programmable Electronic Safety-Related Systems; Part 4: "Definitions and Abbreviations."

IEC 62198. 2001. Project risk management Application Guidelines.

IEEE Std. 610.12-1990. *IEEE Standard Glossary of Software Engineering Terminology* (ANSI American national standard). All rights reserved.

IEEE-Std. 729-1983. *IEEE Standard Glossary of Software Engineering Terminology.*

IEEE Std. 730-1989. *IEEE Standard for Software Quality Assurance Plans* (ANSI American national standard). All rights reserved.

IEEE Std. 830-1993. *IEEE Guide to Software Requirements Specifications* (ANSI American national standard). All rights reserved.

IEEE Std. 982.1-1988. *IEEE Standard Dictionary of Measures to Produce Reliable Software* (ANSI American national standard). All rights reserved.

IEEE Std. 982.2-1988. *IEEE Guide for the Use of IEEE Standard Dictionary of Measures to Produce Reliable Software* (ANSI American national standard). All rights reserved.

IEEE Std. 1002-1987 (Reaff 1992). *IEEE Standard Taxonomy for Software Engineering Standards* (ANSI American national standard). All rights reserved.

IEEE Std. 1016-1987. *IEEE Recommended Practice for Software Design Descriptions* (ANSI American national standard). All rights reserved.

IEEE Std. 1016.1-1993. *IEEE Guide to Software Design Descriptions* (ANSI American national standard). All rights reserved.

IEEE Std. 1028-1988. *IEEE Standard for Software Reviews and Audits* (ANSI American national standard). All rights reserved.

IEEE Std. 1044-1993. *IEEE Standard for Classification of Software Anomalies* (ANSI American national standard). All rights reserved.

IEEE Std. 1061-1992. *IEEE Standard for a Software Quality Metrics Methodology* (ANSI American national standard). All rights reserved.

IEEE Std. 1062-1993. *IEEE Recommended Practice for Software Acquisition* (ANSI American national standard). All rights reserved.

IEEE Std. 1074-1991. *IEEE Standard for Developing Software Life Cycle Processes* (ANSI American national standard). All rights reserved.

IEEE Std. 1219-1992. *Standard for Software Maintenance* (ANSI American national standard). All rights reserved.

IEEE Std. 1228-1994. *IEEE Standard for Software Safety Plans.* All rights reserved.

Imai, M. 1986. *Kaizen: The Key to Japan's Competitive Success.* New York: McGraw-Hill.

Instrument Society of America, ANSI/ISA-S84.01-1996, Application of Safety Instrumented Systems for the Process Industries, 1996.

Instrument Society of America, ANSI/ISA-S88.01-1995, Batch Control; Part 1: "Models and Terminology", 1995.

International Organization for Standardization, ISO/IEC Guide 2, Standardization and related activities—General vocabulary, 1996.

International Organization for Standardization, *ISO 2382-1, Information technology—Vocabulary; part 1: "Fundamental terms,"* 1993.

International Organization for Standardization, ISO 9000-4, *Quality management and quality assurance standards; Part 4: "Guide to dependability programme management,"* 1993 (equal to IEC 300, 1993).

Ireson, G. W., ed. 1966. *Reliability Handbook.* New York: McGraw-Hill (1982 reissue).

Ishikawa, K. 1985. *What is Total Quality Control? The Japanese Way.* Englewood Cliffs, NJ: Prentice Hall Inc.

————. 1986. *Guide to Quality Control.* Tokyo: Asian Productivity Organization.

ISO 2859-1:1989. *Sampling procedures for inspection by attributes—Part 1: Sampling plans indexed by acceptable quality level (AQL) for lot-by-lot inspection.*

ISO 2859-2:1985. *Sampling procedures for inspection by attributes—Part 2: Sampling plans indexed by limiting quality (LQ) for isolated lot inspection.*

ISO 2859-3:1991. *Sampling procedures for inspection by attributes—Part 3: Skip-lot sampling procedures.*

ISO 8402:1986. *Quality vocabulary* (Appendix 1A.3.1.1).

ISO 9000-3:1997. *Quality management and quality assurance standards—Part 3: Guidelines for the Application of ISO 9001:1994 to the development, supply, installation and maintenance of computer software.*

ISO 9000:2000. *Quality management systems—Fundamentals and vocabulary.*

ISO 9001:2000. *Quality management systems—Requirements.*

Johnson, J. 1995. "Chaos: The Dollar Drain of IT Project Failures." *Application Development Trends* 2, no. 1.

Johnson, M. K. 1982. *Statistical Design of Experiments.* Phoenix: Plan Test Associates.

Jones, C. 1986. *Programming Productivity.* New York: McGraw-Hill.

Juran, J. M. 1989. *Juran on Leadership Quality.* New York: The Free Press.

————. 1992. *Juran on Quality by Design: The New Steps for Planning Quality into Goods and Services.* New York: The Free Press.

————. 1995. *Managerial Breakthrough: The Classic Book on Improving Management Performance.* Rev. ed. New York: McGraw-Hill.

Juran, J. M., and A. B. Godfrey. 1999. *Juran's Quality Handbook.* 5th ed. New York: McGraw-Hill.

Juran, J. M., and F. M. Gryna. 1980. *Juran's Quality Planning and Analysis.* 2nd ed. New York: McGraw-Hill.

————. 1988. *Juran's Quality Control Handbook.* 4th ed. New York: McGraw-Hill.

————. 1993. *Juran's Quality Planning and Analysis.* 3rd ed. New York: McGraw-Hill.

Kan, S. 1995. *Metrics and Models in Software Quality Engineering.* Boston, MA: Addison Wesley Longman.

Kaner, C., and D. Pels. 1998. *Bad Software: What to Do When Software Fails.* New York: John Wiley & Sons.

Kaplan, R. S., and D. P. Norton. 1993. "Putting the Balanced Scorecard to Work." *Harvard Business Review* (September–October).

Karch, K. M. 1992/93. "Getting Organizational Buy-in for Benchmarking: Environmental Management at Weyerhaeuser." *National Productivity Review* 12, no. 1.

Karlof, B., and S. Ostblom. 1993. *Benchmarking: A Signpost to Excellence in Quality and Productivity.* New York: John Wiley & Sons.

Karrass, C. L. 1993. *Give and Take: The Complete Guide to Negotiating Strategies and Tactics.* New York: HarperCollins.

Kelvin, W. T., Lord 1889. *Popular Lectures and Addresses.* Vol. 1: 73.

Kerzner, H. 1998. *Project Management: A Systems Approach to Planning, Scheduling, and Controlling.* New York: John Wiley & Sons.

Kessler, S. 1996. *Measuring and Managing Customer Satisfaction: Going for the Gold.* Milwaukee: ASQC Quality Press.

Kirkpatrick, D. 1994. *Evaluating Training Programs: The Four Levels.* San Francisco: Berrett-Koehler.

Kogan Page. 1993. *Management Action Guides: Achieving Goals through Teamwork.* London: Kogan Page.

Kosko, B. 1993. *Fuzzy Thinking.* New York: Hyperion.

Kotler, P. 1972. *Marketing Management Analysis, Planning, and Control.* 2nd ed. Englewood Cliffs, NJ: Prentice Hall.

Kotter, J. P., and L. A. Schlesinger. 1979. "Choosing Strategies for Change." *Harvard Business Review* (March/April).

Kusiak, A. 1993. *Concurrent Engineering Automation, Tools, and Techniques.* New York: John Wiley & Sons.

Laprie, J. C., ed. 1992. *Dependable Computing and Fault-Tolerant Systems, Vol. 5, Dependability: Basic Concepts and Terminology,* Springer-Verlag Wien.

LeBoeuf, M. 1979. *Working Smart: How to Accomplish More in Half the Time.* New York: Warner Books.

Leffler, K. B., 1982. "Ambiguous Changes in Product Quality." *American Economic Review* (December).

Leland, K., and K. Bailey. 1999. *Customer Service for Dummies.* 2nd ed. Foster City, CA: IDG Books Worldwide.

Liker, J. K. 1998. *Becoming Lean. Inside Stories of U.S. Manufacturers.* Portland, OR: Productivity Inc.

Lindsay, W. M., and J. A. Petrick. 1997. *Total Quality and Organization Development.* Delray Beach, FL: St. Lucie Press.

Longman Group. 1995. *Longman Dictionary of Contemporary English.* 3rd ed. Burnt Mill, Harlow England: Longman House.

Lowenstein, M. W. 1995. *Customer Retention: An Integrated Process for Keeping Your Best Customers.* Milwaukee: ASQC Quality Press.

Luther, D. 1994. *A Strategic Planning Process.* Corning, NY: Luther Quality Associates.

Lyu, M. R. 1996. *Handbook of Software Reliability Engineering.* New York: McGraw-Hill.

Mackay, Harvey. 1988. *Swim with the Sharks without Being Eaten Alive.* New York: Ballantine Books.

Malcolm Baldrige National Quality Award (MBNQA) Web site: www//isixsigma.com/ca/Baldrige.

Martin, J. 1997. *Miss Manners' Basic Training: Communication.* New York: Crown Publishers.

Maslow, A. H. 1966. *The Psychology of Science: A Reconnaissance.* Chicago: Regnery.

Masser, W. J. 1957. "The Quality Manager and Quality Costs." *Industrial Quality Control* 14.

McArthur, T. 1981. *Lexicon of Contemporary English.* Burnt Mill, Harlow England: Longman House.

McCall, J., P. Richards, and G. Walters. 1977. *Factors in Software Quality.* Rome, NY: RADC-TR-77-369, US Department of Commerce.

McConnell, S. 1996. *Missing in Action: Information Hiding.* Rome, NY: IEEE Software.

McCormack, M. 1984. *What They Don't Teach You at Harvard Business School.* New York: Bantam Books.

McQuarrie, E. F. 1993. *Customer Visits: Building a Better Market Focus.* San Francisco: Sage Publications.

Mears, P. 1995. *Quality Improvement Tools and Techniques.* New York: McGraw-Hill.

Meyers, F. E. 1999. "Motion and Time Study." In *Lean Manufacturing.* 2nd ed. Upper Saddle River, NJ: Prentice-Hall, Simon & Schuster.

MIL Std. 105E. 1989. *Sampling Procedures and Tables for Inspection by Attributes.* Washington, DC: Department of Defense.

MIL Std. 109. 1994. *Quality Assurance Terms and Definitions.* Washington, DC: Department of Defense

MIL Std. 721. 1981. *Definitions of Terms of Reliability and Maintainability.* Washington, DC: Department of Defense.

MIL Std. 1316E. 1999. *Safety Criteria for Fuse Design.* Washington, DC: Department of Defense.

MIL Std. 1521B. 1985. *Technical Reviews and Audits for Systems, Equipment, and Computer Software.* Washington, DC: Department of Defense.

MIL-STD-1629. 1977. *Procedure for Performing a Failure Mode, Effects and Criticality Analysis.* Washington, D.C.: Department of Defense.

MIL-Q-9858A. 1985. *Quality Program Requirements.*

Mills, C. A. 1988. *The Quality Audit: A Management Evaluation Tool.* New York: McGraw-Hill.

Mintzberg, H. 1990 (digital). *The Manager's Job: Folklore and Fact.* Boston: Harvard Business Review Paperbacks.

Molloy, J. T. 1975. *Dress for Success.* New York: Warner Books.

Montgomery, D. C. 1984. *Design and Analysis of Experiments.* 2nd ed. New York: John Wiley & Sons.

Moss, M. A. 1985. *Designing for Minimal Maintenance Expense.* New York: Marcel Dekker.

Motorola University, OAS100/OAS101. 1996. *Organization Mapping and Analysis: Participant Guide.* Version 2.4. Schaumburg, IL: Motorola.

Murphy's Law. 2002. Day-to-Day Calendar. Kansas-City: Andrews McMeel Publishing.

Myers, G. 1979. *The Art of Software Testing.* New York: John Wiley & Sons.

Myers, P. B., and K. D. Myers. 1987. *Myers-Briggs Type Indicator.* Palo Alto, CA: Consulting Psychologist Press.

Nakajo, T., and H. Kume. 1985. "The Principles of Foolproofing and Their Application in Manufacturing." *Reports of Statistical Application Research* 32, no. 2

NASA George C. Marshall Space Flight Center. 1987. NASA-TM-100311: *Program Risk Analysis Handbook.* Marshall Space Flight Center, AL: NASA.

NATO, ARMP-7. 1996. North Atlantic Treaty Organization (NATO), Military agency for standardization (MAS), ARMP-7, NATO R&M terminology applicable to ARMPs.

Naumann, E., and S. Hoisington. 2001. *Customer-Centered Six Sigma: Linking Customers, Process Improvement, and Financial Results.* Milwaukee: ASQ Quality Press.

Nishiyama, K. 2000. *Doing Business with Japan: Successful Strategies for Intercultural Communication.* Honolulu: University of Hawaii Press.

OREDA. 1992. Offshore Reliability Data handbook, Published by OREDA participants, Pennwell Publishing Company.

Otis, P., J. Carey, et al. 1992. "Quality: Small and Midsize Companies Seize the Challenge Not a Moment Too Soon." *Business Week* (November 30, 1992).

Pande, P. S., R. P. Neuman, and R. R. Cavanagh. 2000. *The Six Sigma Way: How GE, Motorola, and Other Top Companies are Honing Their Performance.* New York: McGraw-Hill.

Park, R. 1996a. "A Manager's Checklist for Validating Software Cost and Schedule Estimates." *American Programmer* (June).

———. 1996b. "Assessing an Organization's Estimating Capabilities." *American Programmer* (July).

Parsowith, B. S. 1995. *Fundamentals of Quality Auditing.* Milwaukee: ASQC Quality Press.

Patentcafe Web site: www.Gibbsgroup.com/inventors_cafe/fraud

Peters, T. 1992. *Liberation Management: Necessary Disorganization for the Nanosecond Nineties.* London: Pan Books.

Phillips, D. 1998. *The Software Project Manager's Handbook: Principles that Work at Work.* Piscataway, NJ: IEEE.

Pirsig, R. M. 1974. *Zen and the Art of Motorcycle Maintenance.* New York: William Morrow & Co.

Poirier, C. C., and W. F. Houser. 1993. *Business Partnering for Continuous Improvement: How to Forge Enduring Alliances among Employees, Suppliers, and Customers.* San Francisco: Berrett-Koehler.

Porter, M. E. 1979. "How Competitive Forces Shape Strategy." *Harvard Business Review* (April).

———. 1985. *Competitive Advantage: Creating and Sustaining Superior Performance.* New York: The Free Press.

Prahalad, C. K., and G. Hamel. 1990. "The Core Competence of the Corporation." *Harvard Business Review* (May–June).

Pressman, R. S. 2001. *Software Engineering: A Practitioner's Approach.* 5th ed. New York: McGraw-Hill.

QS 9000. 1995. *Potential Failure Mode and Effects Analysis* (FMEA). Chrysler Corporation, Ford Motor Company, General Motors Corporation. AIAG.

Raftery, J. 1994. *Risk Analysis in Project Management.* London: E & FN Spon.

Rasiel, E. 1999. *The McKinsey Way.* New York: McGraw-Hill.

Rau, J. G. 1970. *Optimization and Probability in System Engineering.* New York: Van Nostrand Reinhold.

Reliability Analysis Center. 1992. *State-of-the-Art Report Process Action Team Handbook.* Rome, NY: RAC.

Robert, M. 1993. *Strategy Pure and Simple.* New York: McGraw-Hill.

Ross, P. J. 1988. *Taguchi Techniques for Quality Engineering.* New York: McGraw-Hill.

RTCA, D0178B, 1992 Software Considerations in Airborne Systems and Equipment Certification, Advisory Circular, 1992.

Russell, B. 1917. *Introduction to Mathematical Philosophy.* New York: Simon & Schuster.

Russell, J. P. 1990. *The Quality Master Plan: A Quality Strategy for Business Leadership.* Milwaukee: ASQC Quality Press.

Ryan, T. 1992. "Risk Management." *Observer* (June 14): 49.

SA, AS 3563, 1991

Standards Australia, Australian Standard 3563, Software quality management system; Part 1: "Requirements", 1991 (adopted by IEEE as IEEE-Std-1298, 1992).

Salisbury, F. S. 1994. *Developing Managers as Coaches: A Trainer's Guide.* London: McGraw-Hill.

Schaaf, D., and R. Zemke. 1989. *The Service Edge.* New York: Plume.

Schenck, P. 1994. *Identifying and Confirming User Requirements.* Reston, VA: Learning Tree International.

Scholtes, P. R. 1998. *The Leader's Handbook: Making Things Happen, Getting Things Done.* New York: McGraw-Hill.

Scott, C., and D. T. Jaffe. 1991. *Empowerment: A Practical Guide for Success.* Menlo Park, CA: Crisp Publications.

Sea Systems Controllerate Publication No. 83, SSCP 83, Issue 1.0, MOD Project Manager's Guide to C and C++, 1995.

Sea Systems Cotrollerate Publication No. 85, SSCP 85, Issue 2, Joint MOD/Industry Computing Policy for Military Operational Systems, 1995.

Sea Systems Publication No. 84, SSP 84, Issue 1.0, MOD Project Manager's Guide to ADA, March, 1996.

SEI. 1994. *The Capability Maturity Model (CMM): Guidelines for Improving the Software Process.* Boston: Addison Wesley Longman.

SEI. 1997. *Introduction to the Capability Maturity Model (CMM) Course.* Pittsburgh: Carnegie Mellon University, Software Engineering Institute.

SEI Web site: www.sei.cmu.edu.

Senge, P. M. 1990. *The Fifth Discipline.* New York: Doubleday.

Shainin, D. 1984. *Better than Good Old $\bar{X}$ and R Charts Asked by Vendees.* ASQC Quality Congress Transactions, Milwaukee.

Shaw, G. B. 2001. *Man and Superman. A Comedy and a Philosophy.* USA Oklahoma City: Penguin Classics.

Shewhart, W. A. 1986. *Statistical Method from the Viewpoint of Quality Control.* New York: Dover Publications.

Shigeru, M.1988. *Management for Quality Improvement: The Seven New QC Tools.* Cambridge, MA: Productivity Press.

Shook, R. L., and E. Yaverbaum. 1996. *I'll Get Back to You: 156 Ways to Get People to Return Your Phone Calls.* New York: McGraw-Hill

Shtub, A., J. Bard, and S. Globerson. 1994. *Project Management: Engineering, Technology, and Implementation.* Englewood Cliffs, NJ: Prentice-Hall.

SI System Web site: physics nist.gov/Units.html

Silber, L. 1998. *Time Management for the Creative Person.* New York: Three Rivers Press.

Simmerman, S. J. 1993. "Achieving Service Quality Improvements." *Quality Progress* 26, no. 11.

Sinha, M. N. 1993. "Winning Back Angry Customers." *Quality Progress* 26, no. 11.

Smith, A. M. 1993. *Reliability-Centered Maintenance.* New York: McGraw-Hill.

Smith, H. W. 1994. *The Ten Natural Laws of Successful Time and Life Management.* New York: Warner Books.

Smith, D. J. 1981. *Reliability and Maintainability in Perspective, Technical, Management and Commercial Aspects.* New York: John Wiley & Sons.

Spendolini, M. J. 1992. *The Benchmarking Book.* New York: AMACOM.

Spiegel, M. R. 1961. *Shaum's Outline of Theory and Problems of Statistics.* New York: McGraw-Hill.

Stone, B. 2001. *Lessons from an Uncivil Servant.* Istanbul: Turkish Standard Institutions.

Taguchi, G. 1987. *System of Experimental Design.* 2 vols. Dearborn, MI: Unipub/Kraus/American Supplier Institute.

Taguchi, G., and Y. Wu. 1979. *Introduction to Off-Line Quality Control.* Nagoya, Japan: Central Japan Quality Control Association.

Tague, N. R. 1995. *The Quality Toolbox.* Milwaukee: ASQC Quality Press.

Terez, T. 2000. *Twenty-Two Keys to Creating a Meaningful Workplace.* Holbrook, MA: Adams Media.

Thompson, G., and J. Jenkins. 1993. *Verbal Judo: The Gentle Art of Persuasion.* New York: William Morrow.

Thomsett, R. 1995. "Project Pathology: A Study of Project Failures." *American Programmer* (July).

TL 9000. 1999. *Quality System Metrics.* Book 2, Rel 2.5 Committee Draft 3.20. QuEST Forum, September 10.

UK Department of Trade and Industry, ITSEC, Information Technology Security Evaluation Criteria, June 1991.

UK MoD Directorate of Standardization, Defence Standard 00-49, Reliability and maintainability: MOD guide to terminology definitions, 1996.

UK MoD Directorate of Standardization, Interim Defence Standard 00-55, Requirements for safety related software in defence equipment, Issue 2, 1997.

U.S. Air Force. 1988. *Software Risk Abatement.* AFCS/AFLC Pamphlet 800-45.

U.S. Department of Defense, MIL-Std-2167A, Defense system software development, 1988

Van Vleck, T. 1989. *Three Questions about Each Bug You Find.* ACM Software Engineering Notes 14, no. 5: 62–63.

Vincent, J., A. Waters, and J. Sinclair. 1988. *Software Quality Assurance, Vol. 1: Practice and Implementation.* Englewood Cliffs, NJ: Prentice-Hall

Wald, A. 1947. *Sequential Analysis.* New York: John Wiley & Sons.

Walton, K. A. 1999. *Guerrilla Tactics for Getting the Legal Job of Your Dreams.* Chicago: Harcourt Brace Legal and Professional Publications.

Wanner, R. T., and J. Franceschi. 1995. *Reliability Analysis Center (RAC) Business Process Reengineering for Quality Improvement.* Rome, NY: IIT Research Institute.

Watson, G. H. 1993. *Strategic Benchmarking: How to Rate Your Company's Performance against the World's Best.* New York: John Wiley & Sons.

Weinberg, G. 1993. *Quality Software Management, Vol. 2: First-Order Measurement.* New York: Dorset House.

Western Electric. 1956. *Statistical Quality Control Handbook.* Indianapolis: AT&T.

Wheeler, D. J. 2000. *The Process Evaluation Handbook.* Knoxville, Tennessee: SPC Press

Whiteley, R. C. 1991. *The Customer-Driven Company: Moving from Talk to Action.* Reading, MA: Addison Wesley.

Winer, B. J. 1971. *Statistical Principles in Experimental Design.* 2nd ed. New York: McGraw-Hill.

Wortman, B., and D. R. Carlson. 1999. *CQE Primer.* 6th ed. West Terre Haute, IN: Quality Council of Indiana.

Wortman, B., B. Frank, P. Marriott, and C. Warzusen. 2000. *CSQE.* 2nd ed. West Terre Haute, IN: Quality Council of Indiana.

Yamahada, S., M. Ohba, and S. Osaki. 1983. "S-shaped Reliability Growth Modeling for Software Error Detection." *IEEE Transactions on Reliability* R-32.

Yeomans, W. N. 1985. *1,000 Things You Never Learned in Business School.* New York: Penguin Books.

Zahniser, R. 1993. "Design by Walking Around." *Communication of ACM* (October).

Zeithaml, V. A., A. Parasuraman, and L. A. Berry. 1990. *Delivering Service Quality: Balancing Customer Perceptions and Expectations.* New York: The Free Press.

Author Index

A

Adams, S. (*Dilbert*)
    management time fillers, 73
    managerial alternatives, 9
    "out at five" principle, 111
    TQM and stages of evolution, 22
Albrecht, K.
    customer expectations, 129
    customer-driven organizations, 45
Altshuller, G. S.
    inventive principles, 188–89
    inventiveness, 50
ANSI/ASQ Z1.4
    switching procedures, 333
Aristotle
    basis for good talks, 30
Arkin, H.
    sampling, statistical, 214–15
Arter, D. R
    audit phases, 333, 334
    audit preparation phases, 346
Arthur, L. J.
    design quality, 332
    external failure costs, 155
    maintainability metrics, 250
    measurement methods, 209
    measurements—Galileo Galilei, 209
    productivity factors, 128
    productivity measurements, 216
    program performance (software
        efficiency), 38

    software maintainability, 287
    software quality criteria, 316
    software quality facets, 312
    software quality specifications, 294
    successful management, 60–61
ASQ
    code of ethics, 36–37
Atkinson, H.
    enterprises, types of, 10
    project improvements, 91
    quality profit links, 61
    successful companies, strategies
        of, 10
    transforming business into competitive
        gain, 38
Augustine, N.
    Augustine's laws, 102–3
    software, 269

B

Bailey, K.
    human nature, 16
Baker, K., and Baker, S.
    budget equation, 113
    project goals, 153
    project management, 121, 179–80
    project manager categories, 25
    project meeting management, 175
Balsley, R. D.
    conflict resolution, 137, 149

Subject Index

A

acceptable error rate, AER, 335
acceptable performance level, APL, 335
acceptance control limits, 323
acceptance sampling curves, 321
acceptance sampling plan, elements of, 329
accreditation, 350
activities that answer the question "Is it OK?", 350
adaptive control chart, 186
administrative organization responsibilities, 68–69
agenda negotiation, 144
all you have to do, 319
alliances, strategic, 42
analysis, 350
analysis of variance (ANOVA), 196, 212
anomalous process classification, 336
anomalous process steps, 328
ANOVA, analysis of variance, 196, 212
ANOVA, Kruskal-Wallis, 197
ANOVA, two-way, 199
approval, 351
artificial intelligence, 14
ASQ code of ethics, 36–37
assessment, 351
assessment versus evaluation (CMM), 323–24
assignable cause, 118
assists, 292
attribute lifecycle, 156–57

audit, 351
audit classification, 335
audit, configuration, types of, 276
audit findings, 323
audit parties, 330
audit phases, 333, 334
audit preparation phases, 346
audit types, 327, 346
audits and reviews, software, 348–49
auditlike processes, in CMM, 323–24
Augustine's laws, 102–3
availability, 245-46, 257, 329
avoiding software bugs, 287

B

B versus C, 207–8
balanced scorecards, 33, 344
baseline questions, 299
basis for good talks, 30
bathtub curve, 247–48
benchmarking, 17, 121, 126, 140, 145, 172
benchmarking international code, 82
benchmarking partnerships, 163
"best" (B) versus "current" (C), 207–8
better than before, 3
binomial distribution, uses of, 256
brainstorming, 15, 150
budget equation, 113
bug, 273
bug, questions about, 282
bugs, avoiding of, 287